60* Quick Luxury Knits

60 Quick Luxury Knits

EASY, ELEGANT PROJECTS FOR EVERY DAY IN THE **VENEZIA COLLECTION** FROM CASCADE YARNS

THE EDITORS OF
SIXTH&SPRING BOOKS

 sixth&springbooks NEW YORK

 sixth&springbooks

161 Avenue of the Americas, New York, NY 10013
sixthandspringbooks.com

Editorial Director
JOY AQUILINO

Supervising
Patterns Editor
LORI STEINBERG

Vice President
TRISHA MALCOLM

Managing Editor
KRISTY MCGOWAN

Patterns Editors
LORETTA DACHMAN
RENEE LORION
MARGEAU SOBOTI

Publisher
CAROLINE KILMER

Developmental Editor
LISA SILVERMAN

Production Manager
DAVID JOINNIDES

Art Director
DIANE LAMPHRON

Technical Illustrations
LORI STEINBERG

President
ART JOINNIDES

Yarn Editors
JOANNA RADOW
VANESSA PUTT

Proofreader
KRISTIN M. JONES

Chairman
JAY STEIN

Editorial Assistant
JOHANNA LEVY

Photography
JACK DEUTSCH

Art Production
JENNY REED

Fashion Stylist
JOANNA RADOW

Hair & Makeup
SOKPHALLA BAN

Cataloging-in-Publication Data can be found at the Library of Congress.

ISBN: 978-1-936096-76-3

MANUFACTURED IN CHINA

3 5 7 9 10 8 6 4 2

First Edition

CASCADE YARNS
DISTRIBUTOR OF FINE YARN

cascadeyarns.com

contents

Check It Out!

Turn to the inside back cover to find abbreviations, an explanation of skill levels, and even a handy ruler!

Knitting in the Lap of Luxury

We're excited to present the latest entry in our ever-popular 60 Quick Knits series. This time we've introduced a new twist: luxury yarn.

The designs in this book have been created using Cascade Yarns' Venezia Worsted and Venezia Sport, two different weights of the same sumptuously soft blend of merino and silk. The silk content gives the yarn a beautiful sheen and drape, while the merino provides warmth and structure.

The best thing about Venezia is that it's not only luxurious but also affordable—so you can create any of the gorgeous projects in this collection without breaking the bank! Every type of accessory, from shawls to hats to mitts, is included, with plenty of variety for knitters of all styles and skill levels.

Pick up your nicest set of needles and settle in to knit something truly special.

To locate retailers that carry Cascade Venezia, visit cascadeyarns.com.

1

Cable and Eyelet Shawl

Eye-catchingly graphic vertical and diagonal lines are softened
by elegant drape and a pretty edging.

DESIGNED BY ÁGNES KUTAS-KERESZTES

Knitted Measurements
Width at top edge
approx 44"/116.5cm
Height
approx 15"/40cm

Materials
■ 2 3½oz/100g hanks (each approx
307½yd/281m) of Cascade Yarns
Venezia Sport (merino wool/mulberry silk)
in #9817 peacock blue

■ One each sizes 7 and 9 (4.5 and
5.5mm) circular needle, 40"/100cm long,
or size to obtain gauge

■ Size 7 (4.5mm) crochet hook and scrap
yarn, for provisional cast-on

■ Cable needle (cn)

■ Stitch marker

Stitch Glossary
3-st RPC Sl 2 sts to cn and hold to *back*,
k1, sl last st on cn back to LH needle,
hold cn to *front*, p1 from LH needle,
k1 from cn.
5-st RPC Sl 3 sts to cn and hold to *back*,
k2, sl last st on cn back to LH needle,

hold cn to *front*, p1 from LH needle,
k2 from cn.
Inc to 5 ([Yo, k1] 3 times) into same st.

Provisional Cast-On
Using scrap yarn and crochet hook, chain
the number of sts to cast on, plus a few
extra. Cut a tail and pull the tail through
the last chain. With knitting needle and
yarn, pick up and knit the stated number
of sts through the "purl bumps" on the
back of the chain. To remove scrap chain,
when instructed, pull out the tail from
the last crochet st. Gently and slowly pull
on the tail to unravel the crochet sts,
carefully placing each released knit st
on a needle.

Note
Shawl is worked in rows. Circular needle
is used to accommodate large number of
sts. Do not join.

Shawl
Cast on 3 sts using provisional cast-on
method and smaller needle. Work 11
rows in garter st (k every row).

Gauge
15 sts and 28 rows to 4"/10cm after blocking over chart 2 pat using smaller needle.
Take time to check gauge.

Cable and Eyelet Shawl

Next row (RS) Pick up and k 5 sts along side edge, carefully remove provisional cast-on, placing the 3 open sts on LH needle, k these sts—11 sts.
Row 1 (WS) K3, p to last 3 sts, k3.
Row 2 (inc) K3, [kfb] 4 times, k4—15 sts.
Row 3 Rep row 1.
Row 4 (inc) K3, [kfb, kfb, k1] 3 times, k3—21 sts.
Rep row 1 once more.

BEGIN CHART 1
Row 1 (RS) Work to rep line, work st rep 3 times across, work to end of chart. Cont to work chart in this manner until row 10 is complete—51 sts.

BEGIN CHART 2
Row 1 (RS) K3 (garter st edge), [work to rep line, work 5-st rep twice, work to end of chart] 3 times, k3 (garter st edge). Keeping first and last 3 sts of every row in garter st, cont to work chart in this manner until row 10 is complete—81 sts. Rep rows 1–10 six times more, working 2 additional 5-st reps in each section for every 10-row rep—261 sts.
Next (inc) row (RS) [K3, kfb] 27 times, [k3, kfb, k2, kfb] 6 times, [k3, kfb] 27 times, k3—327 sts.
Knit 1 WS row.

BEGIN CHART 3
Row 1 (RS) K3, work to rep line, work 12-st rep 25 times, work to end of chart, k3.
Cont to work chart in this manner until row 17 is complete.
Bind off as foll: P1, *p1, move yarn to back and sl the 2 sts on RH needle back to LH needle, k2tog tbl; rep from * until all sts have been bound off. ■

CHART 1

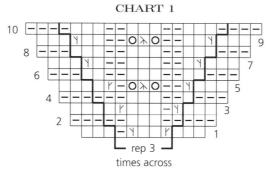

rep 3 times across

CHART 2

5-st rep

STITCH KEY

☐	k on RS, p on WS
☐	p on RS, k on WS
☒	k2tog
☒	SKP
☐	yo
3	p3 on WS
5	k5 on RS, p5 on WS
Y	kfb
ꓭ	pfb
☒	inc to 5 sts
⅄	SK2P
∧	SKP, k1, k2tog
⟋	3-st RPC
⟋	5-st RPC

CHART 3

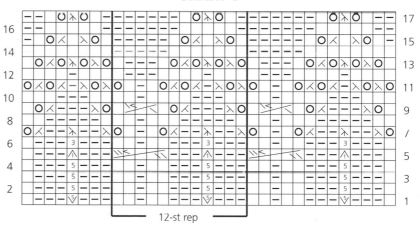

12-st rep

Ribbed Shawl-Collar Cowl

Sporty stripes combined with a shawl collar and I-cord ties make a unique and versatile neck warmer.

DESIGNED BY CHERYL MURRAY

Knitted Measurements
Width
approx 7"/18cm
Length (unstretched)
approx 22¼"/56.5cm

Materials
- 1 3½oz/100g hank (each approx 307½yd/281m) of Cascade Yarns *Venezia Sport* (merino wool/mulberry silk) each in #8400 charcoal (MC) and #177 orchid haze (CC)
- One pair size 5 (3.75mm) needles *or size to obtain gauge*
- Two size 5 (3.75mm) double-pointed needles (dpns) for I-cord ties

K2, P2 Rib
(multiple of 4 sts plus 2)
Row 1 (RS) *K2, p2; rep from * to last 2 sts, k2.
Row 2 *P2, k2; rep from * to last 2 sts, p2.
Rep rows 1 and 2 for k2, p2 rib.

Cowl
With MC, cast on 238 sts. Work in k2, p2 rib for 18 rows.
Row 19 (RS) Change to CC and knit 1 row.
Rows 20–22 Beg with a row 2, work 3 rows in k2, p2 rib.
Row 23 Change to MC and knit 1 row.
Rows 24–26 Beg with a row 2, work 3 rows in k2, p2 rib.
Row 27 Change to CC and knit 1 row.
Rows 28–36 Beg with a row 2, work 9 rows in k2, p2 rib.
Rows 37–40 Rep rows 23–26.
Rows 41–44 Rep rows 19–22.
Next row (RS) Change to MC and knit 1 row.
Work 18 rows in k2, p2 rib.

FIRST TIE
Next row (WS) With dpn, bind off in pat until there are 5 sts on LH needle, k5. *Do not turn work, but slide sts to opposite end of dpn to work the next row from the RS. Pull yarn tightly from end of row, k6. Rep from * for I-cord until tie measures 12"/30.5cm. Do not turn, cont to work as I-cord.
Next (dec) row (RS) [K2tog] 3 times—3 sts. Do not turn, cont to work as I-cord.
Next (dec) row (RS) SK2P. Break yarn and pull through rem st to fasten off.

SECOND TIE
With WS facing, count 34 sts along cast-on edge, with dpn, pick up and k 6 sts in next 6 cast-on sts and complete as for first tie. ■

Gauge
43 sts and 37 rows to 4"/10cm unstretched over k2, p2 rib using size 5 (3.75mm) needles.
Take time to check gauge.

Cable and Eyelet Cap

The warmth and weight of cables strike a balance with airy eyelets in a sweet, simply shaped cap.

DESIGNED BY ALLISON BIRNEY

■◀■■▷

Knitted measurements
Brim circumference 22½"/57cm
Length 8"/20.5cm

Materials
- 1 3½oz/100g hank (each approx 307½yd/281m) of Cascade Yarns *Venezia Sport* (merino wool/mulberry silk) in #177 orchid haze
- One each sizes 5 and 6 (3.75 and 4mm) circular needle, 16"/40cm long, *or size to obtain gauge*
- One set (4) size 6 (4mm) double-pointed needles (dpns)
- Cable needle (cn)
- Stitch marker

Stitch Glossary
4-st LC Sl 2 sts to cn and hold to *front*, k2, k2 from cn.
3-st LPC Sl next st to cn and hold to *front*, p1, k1, k1 from cn.
2-st LC Sl next st to cn and hold to *front*, k1, k1 from cn.
dec 2 P2tog and slip st back to LH needle, pass next st over p2tog and slip resulting st to RH needle—2 sts dec'd.

Cable Pattern
(multiple of 7 sts)
Note Stitch count changes from row to row.
Rnd 1 *K2, yo, k2, p3; rep from * around.
Rnd 2 *K2, yo, p1, yo, k2, dec 2; rep from * around.
Rnd 3 *K2, p1tbl, p1, p1 tbl, k2, p1; rep from * around.
Rnd 4 *K2, p3, k2, p1; rep from * around.
Rnd 5 *K2, dec 2, k2, yo, p1, yo; rep from * around.
Rnd 6 *K1, ssk, k2, p1tbl, p1, p1tbl; rep from * around.
Rnd 7 *K4, yo, p3, yo; rep from * around.
Rnd 8 *4-st LC, p1tbl, p3, p1tbl; rep from * around.
Rnd 9 *K4, ssp, p1, p2tog; rep from * around. Rep rnds 1–9 for cable pat.

Hat
With smaller needle, cast on 140 sts. Join and place marker for beg of rnd, being careful not to twist sts.
Next 3 rnds *K4, p3; rep from * around for k4, p3 rib.
Next (cable) rnd *4-st LC, p3; rep from * around. Work 3 rnds in k4, p3 rib. Rep cable rnd. Change to larger needle and work 1 rnd in k4, p3 rib.

BEGIN CABLE PAT
Work rnd 1 of cable pat, working 7-st rep 20 times around. Cont to work in this manner until rnd 9 is complete. Rep rnds 1–9 four times more.

SHAPE CROWN
Note Change to dpns when there are too few sts to fit comfortably on circular needle.
Next rnd [K2, yo, k2, p1, p2tog] 20 times.
Next (dec) rnd *K2, p1, k2, ssp; rep from * around—120 sts.
Next 2 rnds *K2, p1; rep from * around.
Next (dec) rnd *Ssk, p1, k2tog, p1; rep from * around—80 sts.
Next rnd *K1, p1; rep from * around.
Next (cable) rnd *3-st LPC, p1; rep from * around.
Next (dec) rnd *K2tog, yo, ssk; rep from * around—60 sts.
Next rnd *K1, p1, k1; rep from around.
Next (dec) rnd *Ssk, k1; rep from * around—40 sts.
Next (cable) rnd *2-st LC; rep from * around.
Next 2 (dec) rnds *Ssk; rep from * around—10 sts. Break yarn, leaving a long tail. Thread tail through rem sts and pull tightly to secure. ■

Gauge
25 sts and 36 rnds to 4"/10cm over cable pat after blocking using larger needles.
Take time to check gauge.

Mock Cable & Bell Cowl

Knit stitches and eyelets form delicate mock cables and bell patterns on a reverse-stockinette background.

DESIGNED BY ANGELIQUE DEN BROK

Knitted Measurements
Lower edge circumference
28"/71cm
Upper edge circumference
23"/58.5cm
Length
9"/23cm

Materials
■ 1 3½oz/100g hank (each approx 307½yd/281m) of Cascade Yarns *Venezia Sport* (merino wool/mulberry silk) in #194 cranberry

■ Size 6 (4mm) circular needle, 24"/60cm long, *or size to obtain gauge*

■ Stitch marker

Quick Tip
Because the stitch count changes within the 18–round repeat of the bell panel, keep track by placing markers before and after each repeat of the bell panel.

Stitch Glossary
M4 (K1, [p1, k1] twice) into same st—4 sts inc'd.

Mock Cable Pattern
(over 3 sts)
Rnds 1 and 2 K3.
Rnd 3 K3, pass first st knit over rem 2 sts.
Rnd 4 K1, yo, k1.
Rep rnds 1–4 for mock cable pat.

Bell Panel
(beg and end with 17 sts; stitch count changes within pat)
Rnd 1 P2, M4, [p2, k1tbl] 3 times, p2, M4, p2.
Rnds 2 and 3 P2, k5, [p2, k1tbl] 3 times, p2, k5, p2.
Rnd 4 P2, ssk, k1, k2tog, [p2, k1tbl] 3 times, p2, ssk, k1, k2tog, p2.
Rnd 5 P2, k3, [p2, k1tbl] 3 times, p2, k3, p2.
Rnd 6 P2, S2KP, [p2, k1tbl] 3 times, p2, S2KP, p2.
Rnd 7 P2, k1 tbl, [p2, M5, p2, k1tbl] twice, p2.
Rnds 8 and 9 P2, k1tbl, [p2, k5, p2, k1tbl] twice, p2.

Gauges
21 sts and 32 rows to 4"/10cm over St st after blocking using size 6 (4mm) needles.
1 18-rnd rep of bell panel measures 3¼"/8cm wide and 2"/5cm long after blocking.
Take time to check gauges.

Mock Cable & Bell Cowl

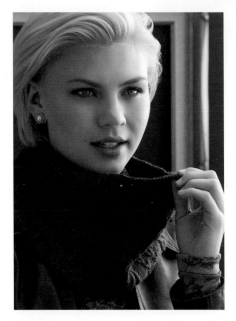

Rnd 10 P2, k1tbl, [p2, ssk, k1, k2tog, p2, k1tbl] twice, p2.
Rnd 11 P2, k1tbl, [p2, k3, p2, k1tbl] twice, p2.
Rnd 12 P2, k1tbl, [p2, S2KP, p2, k1tbl] twice, p2.
Rnd 13 [P2, k1tbl] twice, p2, M4, p2, [k1tbl, p2] twice.
Rnds 14 and 15 [P2, k1tbl] twice, p2, k5, p2, [k1tbl, p2] twice.
Rnd 16 [P2, k1tbl] twice, p2, ssk, k1, k2tog, p2, [k1tbl, p2] twice.
Rnd 17 [P2, k1tbl] twice, p2, k3, p2 [k1tbl, p2] twice.
Rnd 18 [P2, k1tbl] twice, p2, S2KP, p2 [k1tbl, p2] twice.
Rep rnds 1–18 for bell panel.

Cowl
Cast on 155 sts loosely. Place marker and join, being careful not to twist sts.
Set-up rnd *P3, k3, p2, k3, p5, [k1tbl, p2] 5 times; rep from * 4 times more.

BEG PAT
Next rnd [P3, work rnd 1 of mock cable pat over next 3 sts, p2, work rnd 1 of mock cable pat over next 3 sts, p3, work bell panel] 5 times around.
Cont in this way, rep rnds 1–4 of mock cable pat, until rnd 18 of bell panel is complete.
Next (dec) rnd *P2tog, p1, work mock cable pat, p2, work mock cable pat, p1, p2tog, work rnd 1 of bell panel; rep from * 4 times more—10 sts dec'd.
Next rnd *[P2, work mock cable pat] twice, p2, work next rnd of bell panel; rep from * 4 times more.
Cont in this manner until rnd 18 of bell panel is complete.
Next (dec) rnd [P2tog, work mock cable pat, p2, work mock cable pat, p2tog, work rnd 1 of bell panel] 5 times around—10 sts dec'd.
Next rnd [P1, work mock cable pat, p2, work mock cable pat, p1, work next rnd of bell panel] 5 times around.
Cont in this manner until rnd 18 is complete. Rep rnds 1–18 once more.
Next 2 rnds *P1, k3, p2, k3, p3, [k1tbl, p2] 5 times; rep from * around.
Bind off loosely in pat. ■

Slouchy Fair Isle Hat

Show off these whimsical Fair Isle motifs with bright colors,
or use soft neutrals for a completely different look.

DESIGNED BY SHEILA JOYNES

Knitted Measurements
Brim circumference
19"/48cm
Length
9"/23cm

Materials
■ 1 3½oz/100g hank (each approx
307½yd/281m) of Cascade Yarns
Venezia Sport (merino wool/mulberry silk)
each in #178 deep sea (A),
#194 cranberry (B), #189 mushroom (C),
and #179 peacock blue (D)

■ 1 3½oz/100g hank (each approx
307yd/281m) of Cascade Yarns
Venezia Sport Multis (merino
wool/mulberry silk) in #205 teals (E)

■ Size 4 (3.5mm) circular needle,
16"/40.5cm long, *or size to obtain gauge*

■ One set (5) size 4 (3.5mm)
double-pointed needles (dpns)

Hat
With circular needle and B, cast on 140
sts. Place marker for beg of rnd and join,
being careful not to twist sts.
Next rnd *P2 B, k2 E; rep from *
around.
Rep this rnd 9 times more for
corrugated rib.
Knit 1 rnd E.

Next rnd *K1 C, k1 E; rep from *
around.
Knit 1 rnd C.
Next rnd *K1 C, k1 A; rep from *
around.
Next (inc) rnd With A, *k7, M1, rep from
* around—160 sts.

BEGIN CHARTS
Next rnd Work 10-st rep of chart 1
for 16 times around.
Cont to work chart 1 in this manner until
rnd 12 is complete.
Next rnd Work 20-st rep of chart 2
for 8 times around.
Cont to work chart 2 in this manner until
rnd 25 is complete.
Then rep rnds 1–12 of chart 1 once
more.
Next rnd *K1 C, k1 A; rep from *
around.
Knit 1 rnd C.
Next rnd *K1 C, k1 E; rep from *
around.

Gauge
28 sts and 32 rnds to 4"/10cm over chart pats using size 4 (3.5mm) needles.
Take time to check gauge.

Slouchy Fair Isle Hat

CHART 1

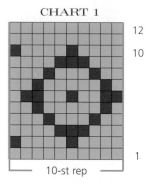

12
10
1

10-st rep

CHART 2

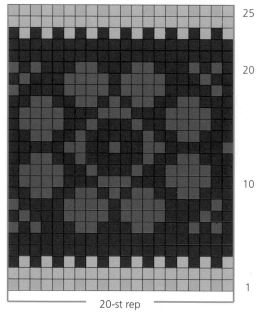

25
20
10
1

20-st rep

SHAPE CROWN

Knit 1 rnd E. Cont with E only to end.
Next (dec) rnd *K6, k2tog; rep from *
around—140 sts.
Knit 1 rnd.
Next (dec) rnd *K5, k2tog; rep from *
around—120 sts.
Knit 2 rnds.
Next (dec) rnd *K4, k2tog; rep from *
around—100 sts.
Knit 2 rnds.
Next (dec) rnd *K3, k2tog; rep from *
around—80 sts.
Knit 1 rnd.
Next (dec) rnd *K2, k2tog; rep from *
around—60 sts.
Next rnd Knit.
Next 2 (dec) rnds *K2tog; rep from *
around—20 sts.

Finishing

Divide sts evenly on 2 dpns and graft
closed using Kitchener st. ∎

COLOR KEY

- Deep sea (A)
- Cranberry (B)
- Mushroom (C)
- Peacock blue (D)

Beads & Bobbles Necklace

Who needs diamonds? Show off this quick-to-knit
beaded neckpiece on your next evening out.

DESIGNED BY KATHY PERRY

Knitted Measurements
Width
approx 2"/5cm
Length along upper edge
17"/43cm

Materials
■ 1 3½oz/100g hank (each approx
307½yd/281m) of Cascade Yarns
Venezia Sport (merino wool/mulberry silk)
each in #173 grey (A) and #120 paint it
black (B)

■ One pair size 5 (3.75mm) needles
or size to obtain gauge

■ Glass roller beads, size 4–6mm with
2–3mm holes, one 25g package or
89 beads in assorted colors

■ Needle with eye to fit through bead

■ Necklace clasp

Stitch Glossary
AB (add bead) Move bead into place
before working next st so that bead sits
between 2 sts.
MB (make bobble) [Kfb, kfb] into same
st, pass sts one at a time over the first st.

Notes
1) Necklace uses approx 25yd/23m of
each color.
2) Necklace is worked from the upper
edge down.
3) Beads are threaded on the yarn
before beginning and moved into place
as called for.

Necklace
Thread 19 beads in colors as desired on
A, cast on 96 sts.
Knit 1 (RS) row.
Next row (WS) K3, *AB, k5; rep from *
to last 3 sts, AB, k3.
Knit 1 row.
Next row K5, *MB, k4; rep from * to
last 6 sts, MB, k5.
Knit 2 rows. Break A.
Thread 24 beads in colors as
desired on B.
Next (faggoting) row With B, k4, *yo,
k2tog, k2; rep from * to last 4 sts, k4.
Next row (WS) K2, AB, k2, *yo, k2tog,
AB, k2; rep from * to end.
Rep faggoting row 8 times more.
Break B.
Thread 46 beads in colors as desired
on A.
Next (picot bind-off) row With A, bind
off 2 sts, *sl st back to LH needle,
cast on 2 sts, AB, bind off 4 sts; rep from
* until all sts are bound off.

Finishing
Attach necklace clasp to side edges. ■

Gauge
22 sts and 24 rows to 4"/10cm over garter st using size 5 (3.75mm) needles.
Take time to check gauge.

Textured Lace Wrap

Lace shows its warm and cozy side in a dramatic oversize scarf perfect for a crisp autumn day.

DESIGNED BY JACQUELINE VAN DILLEN

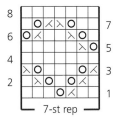

Knitted Measurements
Width
approx 9"/23cm
Length
approx 104"/264cm

Materials
■ 4 3½oz/100g hanks (each approx 219yd/200m) of Cascade Yarns *Venezia Worsted* (merino wool/mulberry silk) in #105 winterfresh

■ One pair size 7 (4.5mm) needles *or size to obtain gauge*

■ Size 7 (4.5mm) crochet hook for fringe

Stitch Glossary
SPP Sl 1 knitwise, p1, pass sl st over to dec 1 st.

Wrap
Cast on 51 sts.
Work 4 rows in garter st (k every row), slipping first st of every row.

BEGIN CHART
Row 1 (RS) Sl 1, work 7-row chart rep 7 times across, k1.
Row 2 (WS) Sl 1, work 7-row chart rep 7 times across, k1.
Cont to work chart in this manner until row 8 is complete. Rep rows 1–8 until scarf measures approx 103 ½"/262.5cm from beg, end with a chart row 8. Cont to sl first st of every row, work 4 rows in garter st. Bind off.

Finishing
FRINGE
Cut 136 strands of yarn, each 11"/28cm long. Hold 4 strands tog and fold in half. With crochet hook, draw loop through edge of scarf. Pull ends through loop and tighten.
Add 17 pieces of fringe to each end of scarf. Trim ends even. ■

STITCH KEY

☐ k on RS, p on WS

⟋ k2tog on RS, p2tog on WS

⟍ SKP on RS, SPP on WS

O yo

7-st rep

Gauge
23 sts and 28 rows to 4"/10cm over chart pat using size 7 (4.5mm) needles. *Take time to check gauge.*

Box Pleat Capelet

This colorblock capelet with a single oversize box pleat
in the front is a study in mod geometry.

DESIGNED BY AMY MICALLEF

■■■□

Knitted Measurements
**Circumference at lower edge
with pleat closed**
approx 40"/101cm
Length
12"/30.5cm

Materials
■ 1 3½oz/100g hank (each approx
307½yd/281m) of Cascade Yarns
Venezia Sport (merino wool/mulberry silk)
each in #194 cranberry (A) and #168
blue spruce (B)

■ One pair each sizes 4 and 5
(3.5 and 3.75mm) needles *or size to
obtain gauge*

■ Stitch holder

■ Bobbins

Seed Stitch
(over an even number of sts)
Row 1 *K1, p1; rep from * to end.
Row 2 K the purl sts and p the knit sts.
Rep row 2 for seed st.

Notes
1) When changing colors, twist strands
on WS to prevent holes in work.
2) Use separate bobbins for each color
section. Do not carry colors across
WS of work.
3) For back: 2 bobbins B, ball of A; for
front: 3 bobbins B, 2 bobbins A.

Back
With smaller needles and B, cast on 15
sts; with A, cast on 82 sts; with 2nd
bobbin of B, cast on 15 sts—112 sts.
Next row (WS) P15 B, p82 A, p15 B.
Next row K15 B, k82 A, k15 B.
Rep last 2 rows once more for color
pat in St st.
Next (turning) row (WS) Cont in color
pat as established, knit.
Change to larger needles.
Work 4 rows in color pat in St st.
Next (joining) row (RS) Fold work at
turning row, with B, *pick up and k 1 st
at cast-on edge and k tog with next st on
LH needle. Cont in color pat and rep
from * to end of row.
Cont in pat for 11 rows more.

SHAPE BODY
Next (body dec) row (RS) With B, k14,
ssk, cont in pat to 1 st before last color
change, with B, k2tog, k14.
Cont in pat, rep body dec row every
4th row 12 times more—86 sts: 15 B,
56 A, 15 B.
Work 1 row in pat.

BEGIN COLOR SHIFT
Next (dec) row (RS) With B, k14, ssk,
k1; with A, k52; with B, k1, k2tog,
k14—84 sts.
Next row P17 B, p50 A, p17 B.
Next (dec) row With B, k16, ssk, k1;
with A, k46; with B, k1, k2tog,
k16—82 sts.
Next row P19 B, p44 A, p19 B. Break A.
Cont in St st with B only, work as foll:
Next (dec) row (RS) Ssk, k to last 2 sts,
k2tog—2 sts dec'd.
Rep dec row every other row 6 times
more—68 sts.
Cont in St st, dec 1 st each side every
row 5 times. Bind off rem 58 sts.

Gauge
22 sts and 30 rows to 4"/10cm over St st using larger needles.
Take time to check gauge.

Box Pleat Capelet

Front

LEFT PANEL
With smaller needles and B, cast on 15 sts; with A, cast on 41 sts—56 sts.
Next row (WS) P41 A, p15 B.
Next row K15 B, k41 A.
Rep last 2 rows once more. Break A and place 56 sts on holder.

RIGHT PANEL
With smaller needles and A, cast on 41 sts; with B, cast on 15 sts—56 sts.
Next row (WS) P15 B, p41 A.
Next row K41 A, k15 B.
Rep last 2 rows once more.
Next (turning) row (WS) K15 B, k41 A; cont with A, cast on 20 sts; with 2nd bobbin of B, cast on 40 sts; with 2nd bobbin of A, cast on 20 sts; with A, k41 from holder; with B, k15 from holder—192 sts.
Change to larger needles.

Next row (RS) K15 B; with A, k40, sl 1, k19, place marker (pm), p1; with B, work in seed st over next 40 sts; with A, p1, pm, k19, sl 1, k40; with B, k15.
Next row P15 B, p60 A, sl marker, k1 A; with B, work in seed st over next 40 sts; k1 A, sl marker, p60 A, p15 B.
Rep last 2 rows once more, slipping markers.
Next (joining) row (RS) Join 56 sts as for back, work in pat over next 80 sts, join rem 56 sts as for back.
Work 1 WS row in pats as established.

BEGIN PLEAT DEC
Row 1 (dec RS) Work in pat to 2 sts before marker, k2tog, sl marker, p1 A, p2tog B, work in seed st to 3 sts before marker, k2tog, p1 A, sl marker, ssk, work in pat to end of row—4 sts dec'd.
Rows 2 and 3 Work even in pat.
Row 4 (dec WS) Work in pat to 2 sts before marker, p2tog tbl, sl marker, k1 A, dec 1 st B, work in seed st to 3 sts before marker, dec 1 st B, k1 A, sl marker, p2tog, work in pat to end of row—4 sts dec'd.
Rows 5 and 6 Work even in pat.
Rep rows 1–6 for pleat dec pat 9 times more, AT THE SAME TIME, when 10 rows have been worked in pleat dec pat, shape body as for back—86 sts when pleat dec and body shaping are complete. (Note: There will no longer be any center sts worked in B when pleat decs are complete.) When pleat dec pat and body dec rows are complete, work color shift and complete as for back. ■

9

Two-Color Cloche

A jaunty cloche gets its style from a colorful crochet-chain band and its structure from doubled yarn and a two-layer brim.

DESIGNED BY ELENA MALO

Knitted Measurements
Head circumference
approx 21"/53.5cm
Length from top of head to edge of brim, at center back
8"/20.5cm

Materials
■ 2 3½oz/100g hanks (each approx 307½yd/281m) of Cascade Yarns *Venezia Sport* (merino wool/mulberry silk) in #190 chocolate (MC)
■ 1 hank in #159 ruby (CC)
■ One pair size 7 (4.5mm) needles *or size to obtain gauge*
■ Size Q (16mm) crochet hook
■ Stitch markers

Short Row Wrap and Turn (w&t)
Knit (purl) side.
1) Wyib, sl next st purlwise.
2) Move yarn between the needles to the front (back).
3) Sl the same st back to LH needle. Turn work, bring yarn to the knit (purl) side between needles. One st is wrapped.
4) When short rows are completed, hide all wraps as foll: work to just before wrapped st. *For knit side:* Insert RH needle under the wrap and knitwise into the wrapped st, k them together. *For purl side:* Insert RH needle from behind into the back loop of the wrap and place it on the LH needle; p wrap tog with st on needle.

Note
MC is used holding 2 strands tog throughout. CC is used holding 1 strand for underside of brim and 2 strands tog for stripe in body of hat.

Cloche
BRIM UNDERSIDE
With 1 strand of CC, cast on 100 sts.
Set-up row (WS) P25, place marker (pm), p50, pm, p25.
Next row (RS) K to first marker, sl marker, knit, inc 10 sts evenly spaced, to next marker, sl marker, knit to end of row—110 sts.
Work 5 rows in St st (k on RS, p on WS), slipping markers every row. Break CC.

BEGIN SHORT ROW SHAPING
Row 1 (RS) Sl first 25 sts, sl marker, join 1 strand of CC, k60, w&t.
Row 2 Sl 1, p to 3 sts before marker, w&t.
Row 3 Sl 1, k to 3 sts before marker, w&t.
Row 4 Sl 1, p to 6 sts before marker, w&t.
Row 5 Sl 1, k to 6 sts before marker, w&t.
Row 6 Sl 1, p to 9 sts before marker, w&t.
Row 7 Sl 1, k to 9 sts before marker.
Break CC.

Gauge
21 sts and 28 rows to 4"/10cm over St st using size 7 (4.5mm) needles and 2 strands of yarn held tog.
Take time to check gauge.

Two-Color Cloche

BRIM

Slip rem sts on LH needle to RH needle. Join 2 strands of MC.

Next row (WS) K110, hiding wraps. Knit 1 WS row. Break yarn.

BEGIN SHORT ROW SHAPING

Row 1 (RS) Sl first 25 sts, sl marker, sl next 9 sts, join 2 strands of MC, k to 9 sts before next marker, w&t.

Row 2 Sl 1, p to 6 sts before marker, w&t.

Row 3 Sl 1, k to 6 sts before marker, w&t.

Row 4 Sl 1, p to 3 sts before marker, w&t.

Row 5 Sl 1, k to 3 sts before marker, w&t.

Row 6 Sl 1, p to marker. Break yarn. Sl rem sts on RH needle to LH needle. Join 2 strands of MC. Work 4 rows in St st.

Next row (RS) K to marker, sl marker, knit, dec 10 sts evenly spaced to next marker, sl marker, k to end—100 sts. Purl 1 row. Break MC.

BEGIN STRIPE

With 2 strands of CC held tog, knit 2 rows.

Cont in CC, work 6 rows in St st. Knit 2 rows. Break CC.

With 2 strands of MC held tog, work in St st until hat measures 2"/5cm from end of stripe, end with a WS row.

SHAPE BACK

Next (dec) row (RS) K8, ssk, k to last 10 sts, k2tog, k8—2 sts dec'd. Purl 1 row. Rep last 2 rows 4 times more—90 sts.

SHAPE CROWN

Next (dec) row (RS) K8, [ssk, k6] 5 times, [k2tog, k6] 5 times, end k2—80 sts. Purl 1 row.

Next (dec) row K1, [ssk, k5] 5 times, ssk, k4, [k2tog, k5] 5 times, end k2tog, k1—68 sts. Purl 1 row.

Next (dec) row K1, [ssk, k4] 5 times, ssk, k2, [k2tog, k4] 5 times, end k2tog, k1—56 sts. Purl 1 row.

Next (dec) row K1, [ssk, k3] 5 times, ssk, [k2tog, k3] 5 times, end k2tog, k1—44 sts. Purl 1 row.

Next (dec) row K1, [ssk, k2] 5 times, [k2tog, k2] 5 times, end k2tog, k1—33 sts. Purl 1 row.

Next (dec) row K1, [ssk, k1] 4 times, ssk, k3tog, [k2tog, k1] 5 times—21 sts. Purl 1 row.

Next (dec) row K1, [ssk] 4 times, [k2tog] 5 times, k1—11 sts. Break yarn, leaving a 20"/51cm tail. Thread tail through rem sts, pull tog tightly and secure end.

Finishing

Sew back seam, matching colors. Fold underside of brim to WS and sew cast-on edge to beg of CC stripe.

HATBAND

With 6 strands of CC and crochet hook, work an even chain approx 21"/53.5cm, or long enough to go around hat loosely. Secure ends on reverse side of chain. Tack chain down along center of stripe.■

Center Back Cable Shawl

Add a new twist to a classic shawl design with a
dramatic cable that bisects the triangle.

DESIGNED BY CANDACE EISNER STRICK

Knitted Measurements
Width (wingspan)
30"/76
Length
16¼"/41cm

Materials
■ 3 3½oz/100g hanks (each approx
307½yd/281m) of Cascade Yarns
Venezia Sport Multis (merino
wool/mulberry silk) in #203 wines

■ Size 5 (3.75mm) circular needle,
24"/60cm long, *or size to obtain gauge*

■ Size F/5 (3.75mm) crochet hook

■ Scrap yarn for provisional cast-on

■ Cable needle (cn)

■ Stitch markers

Stitch Glossary
CE (chain edge) Sl 1 st purlwise wyif.
4-st RC Sl 2 sts to cn and hold to *back*,
k2, k2 from cn.
4-st LC Sl 2 sts to cn and hold to *front*,
k2, k2 from cn.

Welt Pattern
(any number of sts)
Row 1 (WS) Knit.
Row 2 Purl.
Rows 3 and 4 Knit.
Row 5 Purl.
Row 6 Knit.
Rep rows 1–6 for welt pat.

Center Cable Pattern
(over 12 sts)
Row 1 (WS) P12.
Row 2 K2, 4-st RC, 4-st LC, k2.
Rows 3, 5, and 7 Rep row 1.
Row 4 4-st RC, k4, 4-st LC.
Row 6 K2, 4-st LC, 4-st RC, k2.
Row 8 K4, 4-st RC, k4.
Rep rows 1–8 for center cable pat.

Provisional Cast-on
With scrap yarn and crochet hook, ch
the number of sts to cast on plus a few
extra. Cut a tail and pull the tail through
the last chain. With knitting needle and
yarn, pick up and knit the stated number
of sts through the "purl bumps" on the
back of the chain. To remove scrap yarn
chain, when instructed, pull out the tail
from the last crochet stitch. Gently and
slowly pull on the tail to unravel the
crochet stitches, carefully placing each
released knit stitch on a needle.

Gauge
24 sts and 45 rows to 4"/10cm over welt pat before steaming, using size 5 (3.75mm) needles.
Take time to check gauge.

Center Back Cable Shawl

Notes

1) Shawl is worked from the tab that forms the back neck down to the pointed tip.

2) Circular needle is used to accommodate large number of sts. Do not join.

Shawl

TAB

Cast on 4 sts using provisional cast-on method. Knit 1 row.

Next row CE, k3.
Rep last row 27 times more. Do not turn. Pick up and k 13 sts in the sl sts along the LH edge of tab. Carefully remove provisional cast-on and cont around, k3—20 sts.

Row 1 (WS) CE, k2 (for border), k1, place marker (pm), p12 (for center cable), pm, k1, k3 (for border).

Row 2 CE, k2, yo, kfb, yo, sl marker, work row 2 of center cable pat to marker, sl marker, yo, kfb, yo, k3—6 sts inc'd.

Row 3 CE, k2, work row 3 of welt pat to marker, sl marker, work row 3 of center cable pat to marker, sl marker, work in welt pat to last 3 sts, k3.

Row 4 CE, k2, yo, kfb, work next row of welt pat to next marker, yo, sl marker, work next row of cable pat to marker, sl marker, yo, work welt pat to last 4 sts, kfb, yo, k3—6 sts inc'd.
Cont to inc sts every other row in this manner and rep rows 1–8 of center cable pat and rows 1–6 of welt pat on each side of cable pat until there are 202 sts on each side of center cable—416 sts. End with a RS row 6 of welt pat.

LOWER BORDER

Next row (WS) K to marker, sl marker, k3, k2tog, k2, k2tog, k3, sl marker, k to end of row—414 sts.
Work 3 rows in rev St st (p on RS, k on WS). Bind off on WS knitwise.

Finishing

Lightly steam to relax welting. Do not straighten upper edge, but keep the deep curve so that shawl sits nicely on shoulders. ■

Diamonds & Bobbles Scarf

Zigzagging cables form diamonds around bobbles in the centerpiece of this charming variation on the ribbed scarf.

DESIGNED BY ANNA AL

Knitted Measurements
Width
approx 7"/18cm
Length
approx 67"/170cm

Materials
■ 2 3½oz/100g hanks (each approx 307 ½yd/281m) of Cascade Yarns *Venezia Sport Multis* (merino wool/mulberry silk) in #202 denim

■ One pair size 7 (4.5mm) needles *or size to obtain gauge*

■ Cable needle (cn)

Stitch Glossary
Wrap 3 Sl next 3 sts with yarn in back, bring yarn to front, sl same 3 sts back to LH needle, k1, yo, k2tog tbl.
2-st RPC Sl next st to cn and hold to *back*, k1 tbl, p1 from cn.
2-st LPC Sl next st to cn and hold to *front*, p1, k1 tbl from cn.
3-st RPC Sl next st to cn and hold to *back*, k2 tbl, p1 from cn.
3-st LPC Sl 2 sts to cn and hold to *front*, p1, k2 tbl from cn.
5-st RC Sl 2 sts to cn and hold to *back*, k3 tbl, k2 from cn.
5-st LC Sl 3 sts to cn and hold to *front*, k2, k3 tbl from cn.
MB (make bobble) [K1, p1, k1, p1, k1] in same st, turn; p2tog, p1, p2tog, turn; SK2P.

Cable Pattern 1
(over 21 sts)
Row 1 (RS) P4, [3-st RPC] twice, p1, [3-st LPC] twice, p4.
Row 2 and all WS rows K the knit sts and p1 tbl the purl sts.
Row 3 P3, [3-st RPC] twice, p3, [3-st LPC] twice, p3.
Row 5 P2, [3-st RPC] twice, p5, [3-st LPC] twice, p2.
Row 7 P2, 5-st LC, p3, MB, p3, 5-st RC, p2.
Row 9 P2, [3-st LPC] twice, p5, [3-st RPC] twice, p2.

Gauge
21 sts and 27 rows to 4"/10cm over St st using size 7 (4.5mm) needles.
Take time to check gauge.

Diamonds & Bobbles Scarf

Row 11 P3, [3-st LPC] twice, p3, [3-st RPC] twice, p3.
Row 13 P4, [3-st LPC] twice, p1, [3-st RPC] twice, p4.
Row 14 Rep row 2.
Rep rows 1–14 for cable pat 1.

Cable Pattern 2
(over 7 sts)
Row 1 (RS) P2, wrap 3, p2.
Row 2 K2, p3, k2.
Row 3 P2, k3, p2.
Row 4 Rep row 2.
Rows 5–22 Rep rows 1–4 for 4 times more, then rep rows 1 and 2.
Row 23 P1, 2-st RPC, k1 tbl, 2-st LPC, p1.
Row 24 K1, [p1 tbl, k1] 3 times.
Row 25 P1, [k1 tbl, p1] 3 times.
Rows 26–49 Rep rows 24 and 25 for 13 times more.

Row 50 Rep row 24.
Row 51 P1, 2-st LPC, k1 tbl, 2-st RPC, p1.
Row 52 Rep row 2.
Rep rows 1–52 for cable pat 2.

Scarf
Cast on 57 sts.
Row 1 (RS) [K1, p1] twice, p2, k1, p1, k1, p2, [p1, k1] 3 times, p6, k2, [p1, k2] 3 times, p6, [k1, p1] 3 times, p2, k1, p1, k1, p2, [p1, k1] twice.
Row 2 K2, p1, k3, p1, k1, p1, k2, [k1, p1] 3 times, k6, [p2, k1] 4 times, k5, [p1, k1] 3 times, k2, p1, k1, p1, k3, p1, k2.
Rep rows 1 and 2 for 8 times more for rib.

BEGIN CABLE PATS
Next row (RS) [K1, p1] twice, work row 1 of cable pat 2 over next 7 sts, work row 27 of cable pat 2 over next 7 sts, work row 1 of cable pat 1 over next 21 sts, work row 27 of cable pat 2 over next 7 sts, work row 1 of cable pat 2 over next 7 sts, [p1, k1] twice.
Next row (WS) K2, p1, k1, work row 2 of cable pat 2 over next 7 sts, work row 28 of cable pat 2 over next 7 sts, work row 2 of cable pat 1 over next 21 sts, work row 28 of cable pat 2 over next 7 sts, work row 2 of cable pat 2 over next 7 sts, k1, p1, k2.
Cont to work pats in this way until work measures approx 65"/165cm, end with a row 14 of cable pat 1.
Work rib as for beg of scarf.
Bind off in rib. ∎

Wavy Ribbed Hat

Ribs that begin at the brim are broken up by dropped stitches as they undulate toward the crown.

DESIGNED BY RACHEL MAURER

Knitted Measurements

Brim circumference
21¼"/54cm
Length with brim folded
8"/20.5cm

Materials

■ 1 3½oz/100g hank (each approx 307½yd/281m) of Cascade Yarns *Venezia Sport* (merino wool/mulberry silk) in #173 grey

■ Size 3 (3.25mm) circular needle, 16"/40cm long, *or size to obtain gauge*

■ One set (4) size 3 (3.25mm) double-pointed needles (dpns)

■ Stitch markers

Stitch Glossary

M1 p-st Insert needle from front to back under strand between last st worked and next st on LH needle. Purl into back loop to twist st.

K3, P2 Rib

(multiple of 5 sts)
Rnd 1 *K3, p2; rep from * around.
Rep rnd 1 for k3, p2 rib.

Wavy Rib Pattern

(multiple of 8 sts)
Note St multiple changes to 9 sts in rnds 1 and 8 and back to 8 in rnds 7 and 17.
Rnd 1 *K2, p1, M1 p-st, p1, k2, p2; rep from * around.
Rnds 2–6 *K2, p3, k2, p2; rep from * around.
Rnd 7 *K2, p1, drop next st and let unravel, p1, k2, p2; rep from * around.
Rnd 8 *K2, p2, k2, p1, m1 p-st, p1; rep from * around.
Rnds 9–13 *K2, p2, k2, p3; rep from * around.

Rnd 14 *K2, p2, k2, p1, drop next st and let unravel down; rep from * around.
Rep rnds 1–14 for wavy rib pat.

Hat

RIBBED BRIM
Cast on 160 sts. Place marker for beg of rnd and join, being careful not to twist sts. Work in k3, p2 rib for 2"/5cm.
Next (dec) rnd *Ssk, k1, p2; rep from * around—128 sts.

BEGIN WAVY RIB PAT
Work in wavy rib pat until piece measures 9"/23cm from beg, end with a rnd 7 or 14.

SHAPE CROWN
Rnd 1 *K2, p2tog; rep from * around—96 sts.
Rnds 2–3 *K2, p1; rep from * around.
Rnd 4 K2, *k2tog, k1; rep from * around, end k2tog with first st of rnd—64 sts.
Rnds 5–6 Knit.
Rnd 7 *K2tog, rep from * around—32 sts.
Rnds 8–9 Knit.
Break yarn, leaving a long tail. Thread tail through rem sts and pull tightly to secure.

Finishing

Fold ribbed brim to RS to wear. ■

Gauge

30 sts and 33 rnds to 4"/10cm over wavy rib pat using size 3 (3.25mm) needles. *Take time to check gauge.*

Cabled Wave Scarf

Densely textured cables, soft curves at the ends, and alternating panels at the sides evoke rolling waves.

DESIGNED BY DANIELLE CHAISON

Knitted Measurements
Width
approx 7"/18cm
Length
approx 66"/167.5cm

Materials
- 3 3½oz/100g hanks (each approx 307½yd/281m) of Cascade Yarns *Venezia Sport* (merino wool/mulberry silk) in #101 white heaven
- One pair size 7 (4.5mm) needles *or size to obtain gauge*
- Cable needle (cn)

Stitch Glossary
8-st RC Sl 4 sts to cn and hold to *back*, k4, k4 from cn.
8-st LC Sl 4 sts to cn and hold to *front*, k4, k4 from cn.

Scarf
Cast on 64 sts. Knit 3 rows.
Next row (RS) P7, k1, p to last 8 sts, k1, p7.
Next row K the knit sts and p the purl sts.
Rep last 2 rows twice more.
Next (set-up) row P8, [8-st LC] 6 times, p8.
Next row K the knit sts and p the purl sts.

BEGIN CABLE PAT
Row 1 (RS) Sl 1, k6, p1, k to last 8 sts, p1, k7.
Row 2 and all WS rows Sl 1, k the knit sts and p the purl sts to end.
Row 3 Sl 1, k6, p1, *8-st LC; rep from * to last 8 sts, p1, k7.
Row 5 Rep row 1.
Row 7 Sl 1, k6, p1, k4, *8-st RC; rep from * to last 12 sts, k4, p1, k7.
Row 9 Sl 1, p7, k to last 8 sts, p8.
Row 11 Sl 1, p7, *8-st LC; rep from * to last 8 sts, p8.
Row 13 Sl 1, p7, k to last 8 sts, p8.
Row 15 Sl 1, p7, *8-st RC; rep from * to last 8 sts, p8.
Row 16 Sl 1, k to end.

Rep rows 1–16 for 32 times more, piece measures approx 32"/81cm from beg, end with a row 8.
Next 2 rows K the knit sts and p the purl sts.

BEGIN REVERSE CABLE PAT
Row 1 (RS) Sl 1, k6, p1, k to last 8 sts, p1, k7.
Row 2 and all WS rows Sl 1, k the knit sts and p the purl sts to end.
Row 3 Sl 1, k6, p1, *8-st RC; rep from * to last 8 sts, p1, k7.
Row 5 Rep row 1.
Row 7 Sl 1, k6, p1, k4, *8-st LC; rep from * to last 12 sts, k4, p1, k7.
Row 9 Sl 1 p7, k to last 8 sts, p8.
Row 11 Sl 1 p7, *8-st RC; rep from * to last 8 sts, p8.
Row 13 Sl 1 p7, k to last 8 sts, p8.
Row 15 Sl 1, p7, *8-st LC; rep from * to last 8 sts, p8.
Row 16 Sl 1, k to end.
Rep rows 1–16 for 32 times more. Rep rows 1–6 once more.
Next row (RS) P8, k to last 8 sts, p8.
Next row K the knit sts and p the purl sts.
Knit 3 rows. Bind off. ∎

Gauge
22 sts and 32 rows to 4"/10cm over pat st using size 7 (4.5mm) needles.
Take time to check gauge.

Striped and Buttoned Hat

Blend sporty and sophisticated in a quick knit with narrow stripes and a single button at the brim.

DESIGNED BY RACHEL RODEN

Knitted Measurements
Brim circumference
22"/56cm
Length
7½"/19cm

Materials
■ 1 3½oz/100g hank (each approx 307½yd/281m) of Cascade Yarns *Venezia Sport* (merino wool/mulberry silk) each in #132 mouse (A), #120 paint it black (B), and #160 ginger (C)

■ One each sizes 3 and 5 (3.25 and 3.75mm) circular needle, 16"/40cm long, *or size to obtain gauge*

■ One set (4) size 5 (3.75mm) double-pointed needles (dpns)

■ One ⅞"/22mm button

■ Stitch markers

K2, P2 Rib
(multiple of 4 sts)
Row 1 (RS) *K2, p2; rep from * around.
Row 2 K the knit sts and p the purl sts.
Rep row 2 for k2, p2 rib.

Stripe Sequence
In St st work 3 rows A, 2 rows B, 1 row C, 1 row A, 2 rows B, 3 rows C. Rep these 12 rows for stripe sequence.

Notes
1) Ribbed brim is worked back and forth in rows. When brim is complete, piece is joined and hat is worked in the round.
2) Carry colors up the hat at beg of rnd; do not cut yarn for each stripe.
3) Change to dpns when there are too few sts to fit comfortably on circular needle.

Hat
With C and smaller needle, cast on 136 sts. Do not join. Work 4 rows in k2, p2 rib.
Next (buttonhole) row (RS) K2, p2, bind off 2 sts, cont in pat as established to end of row.
Next row (WS) Work in pat to bound-off sts, cast on 2 sts, work to end of row. Cont in k2, p2 rib until brim measures 1¼"/3cm from beg, end with a WS row.
Next row (RS) Bind off 10 sts, work in rib to end of row—126 sts. Change to larger needle, place marker for beg of rnd and join. Knit 1 rnd.

BEGIN STRIPE SEQUENCE
Work in stripe sequence until hat measures 5½"/14cm from beg.

SHAPE CROWN
Set-up rnd [K12, k2tog, pm] 8 times, k12, k2tog—117 sts. Knit 1 rnd, slipping markers.
Next (dec) rnd [K to 2 sts before next marker, k2tog, sl marker] 9 times—9 sts dec'd.
Rep dec rnd every other rnd 4 times more—72 sts. Rep dec rnd every rnd 7 times more—9 sts. Break yarn, leaving a long tail. Thread tail through open sts twice and pull tightly to secure.

Finishing
Sew on button to correspond to buttonhole. ■

Gauge
22 sts and 32 rnds to 4"/10cm over St st using size 5 (3.75mm) needles.
Take time to check gauge.

15

Collared Cape

This chic tailored cape with a foldover ribbed collar is the perfect extra layer for a brisk fall day.

DESIGNED BY FLEURTJE ELIZA

◧ ■ ▫ ▭

Knitted Measurements
Width at lower edge
52"/132cm
Width at collar
18"/45.5cm
Length
18"/45.5cm

Materials
■ 3 3½oz/100g hanks (each approx 219yd/200m) of Cascade Yarns *Venezia Worsted* (merino wool/mulberry silk) in #127 forest

■ One pair size 10 (6mm) needles *or size to obtain gauge*

■ Stitch markers

Stitch Glossary
k1-b Knit 1 st in the row below the next st on the LH needle.

Pattern Stitch
(multiple of 4 sts plus 2)
Set-up row (WS) Knit.
Row 1 (RS) *K2, [k1-b] twice, k2; rep from * to end.
Row 2 and all WS rows Knit.
Row 3 Rep row 1.
Row 5 [K1-b] twice, *k2, [k1-b] twice; rep from * to end.
Row 7 Rep row 5.
Row 8 Rep row 2.
Rep rows 1–8 for pat st.

Cape
Cast on 140 sts. Knit 1 WS row.
Next row (RS) K1, work row 1 of pat st over next 138 sts, k1.
Next row (WS) K1, work row 2 of pat st over next 138 sts, k1.
Cont in this manner until row 8 of pat st is complete. Rep rows 1–8 of pat st until piece measures 11"/28 cm from beg, end with a WS row. Place marker in both ends of this row.

SHAPE COLLAR
Next (dec) row (RS) K1, *p2tog, k2; rep from * to last 3 sts, p2tog, k1—105 sts.
Next row K2, *p2, k1; rep from * to last st, k1.
Next 2 rows Keeping first and last st of each row in garter st (k every row), k the knit sts and p the purl sts as they appear.
Next (dec) row (RS) K1, *p, k2tog, rep from * to last 2 sts, p1, k1—71 sts.
Next row K1, *p1, k1; rep from * to end.
Next row Keeping first and last st of each row in garter st, k the knit sts and p the purl sts as they appear for k1, p1 rib. Cont in k1, p1 rib as established until collar measures 12"/30.5cm from marker. Bind off.

Finishing
Fold collar to WS and sew bound-off edge to marked row. Sew sides of collar along garter st edges.
Sew button to left side of cape just below collar (use photo as guide).
Push button through a stitch on right side of cape for buttonhole. ■

Gauge
11 sts and 32 rows to 4"/10cm over pat st using size 10 (6mm) needles.
Take time to check gauge.

Graphic Multicolor Mitts

Bands of sloping stripes worked in tonal colors lend modern flair
to dramatically long arm warmers.

DESIGNED BY CHERYL MURRAY

Finished Measurements
Hand circumference
7½"/19cm
Length
13"/33cm

Materials
■ 1 3½oz/100g hank (each approx 307½yd/281m) of Cascade Yarns *Venezia Sport* (merino wool/mulberry silk) each in #196 lagoon (A), #188 deep forest (B), #197 spring green (C), #187 sage (D), #179 peacock blue (E), #130 denim (F), #159 ruby (G), #193 power pink (H), and #194 cranberry (I)

■ One set (5) size 3 (3.25) double-pointed needles (dpns)

■ Scrap yarn

K1, P1 Rib
(over an even number of sts)
Rnd 1 *K1, p1; rep from * around.
Rep rnd 1 for k1, p1 rib.

Left Mitt
With A, cast on 80 sts. Join and place marker (pm) for beg of rnd, being careful not to twist sts. Divide sts evenly on 4 dpns.
Work 9 rnds in k1, p1 rib.

SHAPE CUFF
Next (dec) rnd K1, ssk, work in rib to last 2 sts, k2tog—2 sts dec'd.
Cont in rib as established and rep dec rnd every 5th rnd 9 times more, working decs into rib pat—60 sts.
Work even in rib until cuff measures 8"/20.5cm from beg. Knit 1 rnd.

HAND
Rnd 1 Work 12-st rep of chart 1 twice, then rep sts 1–6, pm, work rnd 1 of chart 2, pm, beg with st 6 of chart 1, work to end of chart, then work 12-st rep twice—61 sts.
Cont to work charts in this manner, sl markers every rnd, until rnd 28 is complete.

Next rnd Cont in chart pat to marker, remove marker, place next 19 sts on scrap yarn for thumb, remove next marker, cont in chart 1 pat as established—60 sts in rnd. Cont in chart pat until rnd 40 is complete.
With A, knit one row.
Work 10 rnds in k1, p1 rib. Bind off loosely in rib.

THUMB
Place 19 thumb sts evenly on dpns.
Next rnd With A, pick up and k 3 sts along thumb opening, k19—22 sts. Pm for beg of rnd.
Next rnd Work in k1, p1 rib, dec 2 sts evenly around—20 sts.
Work in k1, p1 rib for 6 rnds more. Bind off loosely in rib.

Right Mitt
Work as for left mitt. ■

Gauge
30 sts and 40 rnds to 4"/10cm over chart 1 pat using size 3 (3.25mm) needles.
Take time to check gauge.

Graphic Multicolor Mitts

CHART 1

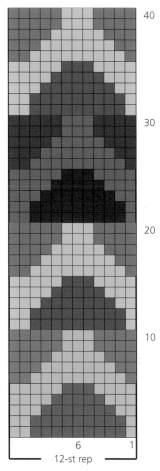

40

30

20

10

6   1

12-st rep

CHART 2

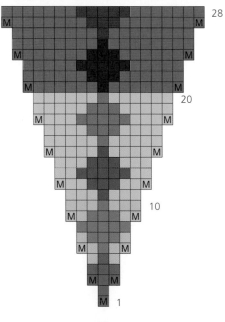

28

20

10

1

COLOR KEY

- ☐ Lagoon (A)
- ■ Deep forest (B)
- ☐ Spring green (C)
- ■ Sage (D)
- ■ Peacock blue (E)
- ■ Denim (F)
- ■ Ruby (G)
- ■ Power pink (H)
- ■ Cranberry (I)
- M M1 in color indicated

Lacy Leaves Snood

Face the autumn chill with lace that has warmth and structure,
thanks to worsted-weight yarn and I-cord edges.

DESIGNED BY HALLEH TEHRANIFAR

Knitted Measurements
Circumference at lower edge
42"/106.5cm
Length 12"/30.5cm

Materials
■ 1 3½oz/100g hank (each approx
219yd/200m) of Cascade Yarns
Venezia Worsted (merino wool/mulberry
silk) in #161 turquoise
■ Size 6 (4mm) circular needle, 24"/60cm
long, *or size to obtain gauge*
■ Two size 6 (4mm) double-pointed
needles (dpns) for I-cord
■ Size G/6 (4mm) crochet hook
■ Scrap yarn
■ Stitch marker

Provisional Cast-on
With scrap yarn and crochet hook, chain
the number of sts to cast on, plus a few
extra. Cut a tail and pull the tail through
the last chain. With knitting needle and
yarn, pick up and knit the stated number
of sts through the "purl bumps" on the
back of the chain. To remove scrap chain,
when instructed, pull out the tail from
the last crochet st. Gently and slowly
pull on the tail to unravel the crochet sts,
carefully placing each released knit
st on a needle.

Snood
Cast on 187 sts, using provisional cast-on
method. Place marker for beg of rnd and
join, being careful not to twist sts.

BEGIN CHART
Rnd 1 Work 17-st rep 11 times around.
Cont to work chart in this manner
until rnd 20 is complete.
Rep rnds 1–20 twice more, then
rep rnds 1–8 once.

SHAPE UPPER EDGE
Rnd 1 (dec) *K2, yo, S2KP, yo, k7, yo
S2KP, SKP, yo; rep from * 10 times
more—176 sts.
Rnd 2 and all even-numbered rnds Knit.
Rnd 3 (dec) *K2, [yo, k2tog] twice, k5,
SKP, yo, SK2P, yo; rep from * 10 times
more—165 sts.
Rnd 5 *K2, [yo, k2tog] twice, k5, [SKP,
yo] twice; rep from * 10 times more.
Rnds 7 and 9 Rep rnd 5.
Rnd 11 (dec) *K2, [yo, k2tog] twice, k1,
SK2P, k1, [SKP, yo] twice; rep from * 10
times more—143 sts.
Rnd 13 *K2, [yo, k2tog] twice, k3, [SKP,

Gauge
19 sts and 26 rnds to 4"/10cm over chart pat using size 6 (4mm) needles.
Take time to check gauge.

17
Lacy Leaves Snood

yo] twice; rep from * 10 times more.
Knit 1 rnd.

BEGIN I-CORD BIND-OFF
Cast on 3 sts to beg of rnd.
Next rnd *With dpn, k2, k2tog tbl (one
I-cord st with 1 st from body of snood);
slide 3 sts just worked to opposite end of
dpn to work next row from RS. Pull yarn
tightly from beg of row; rep from * until
all snood sts have been worked.
Bind off rem 3 sts.

Finishing
Carefully remove scrap yarn from
provisional cast-on and place open sts
on circular needle. Work I-cord bind-off
as for upper edge. ∎

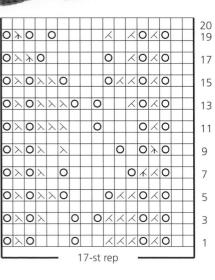

17-st rep

50

18

Fair Isle Cape

A graphic lovebird motif adds tribal flair to this dramatic cape
knit in two panels and seamed together.

DESIGNED BY YOKO HATTA

■■■◻

Knitted Measurements
Width including ribbed edges
21"/53.5cm
**Length from center back
to lower edge**
28"/71cm

Materials
■ 5 3½oz/100g hanks (each approx
219yd/200m) of Cascade Yarns *Venezia
Worsted* (merino wool/mulberry silk) in
#174 mulberry (A)

■ 1 hank in #177 orchid haze (B)

■ One pair each sizes 3, 6, and 7
(3.25, 4, and 4.5mm) needles *or size to
obtain gauge*

■ Size 3 (3.25mm) circular needle,
32"/80cm long

■ Spare size 6 (4mm) needle for
3-needle bind-off

■ Size G/6 (4mm) crochet hook for
button loop

■ One 1¾"/44mm button

K2, P2 Rib
(multiple of 4 sts plus 2)
Row 1 (RS) *K2, p2; rep from * to last 2
sts, k2.
Row 2 P2, *k2, p2; rep from * to end.
Rep rows 1 and 2 for k2, p2 rib.

3-Needle Bind-Off
1) Hold right sides of pieces together
on 2 needles. Insert 3rd needle knitwise
into first st of each needle, and wrap
yarn knitwise.
2) Knit these 2 sts together and slip them
off the needles. *Knit the next 2 sts
together in the same manner.
3) Slip first st on 3rd needle over 2nd st
and off needle. Rep from * in step 2
across row until all sts are bound off.

Note
Work selvage sts in St st throughout.

Cape
LEFT PANEL
With size 3 (3.25mm) needles and A,
cast on 100 sts.
Next row K1 (selvage), *k2, p2; rep from
* to last 3 sts, k2, k1 (selvage).
Keeping first and last st of each row in

St st, cont in k2, p2 rib as established
until 14 rows are complete.
Next row (RS) K2tog, k to end—99 sts.
Purl 1 row.
Change to size 7 (4.5mm) needles.
Next row *K1 with B, k1 with A; rep
from * to last st, k1 with B.
Next row *P1 with A, p1 with B; rep
from * to last st, p1 with A.
Work 2 rows in A.

BEGIN CHART 1
Next row (RS) K1 in next color (selvage),
work 32-st rep 3 times, work to end
of chart, k1 in last color used (selvage).
Cont to work chart in this manner until
row 16 is complete.
With A, knit 1 row.

BEGIN CHART 2
Next row (WS) P1, work 4-st rep
24 times, p1 in last color used.
Next row (WS) K1, work 4-st rep
24 times, work to end of chart, k1 in
last color used.
Cont to work chart in this manner until
row 6 is complete.
With A, work 2 rows.

Gauges
22 sts and 29 rows to 4"/10cm over St st using size 6 (4mm) needles.
22 sts and 28 rows to 4"/10cm over chart pats using size 7 (4.5mm) needles.
Take time to check gauges.

Fair Isle Cape

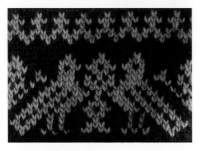

COLOR KEY

 Mulberry (A)

 Orchid haze (B)

CHART 1

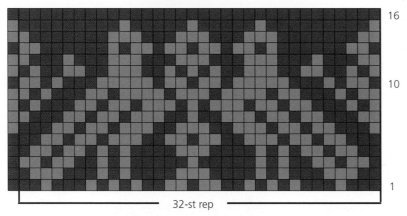

16

10

1

32-st rep

CHART 2

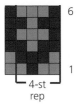

6

1

4-st
rep

CHART 3

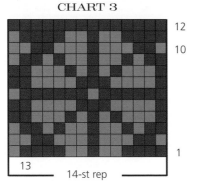

12

10

1

13

14-st rep

CHART 4

6

1

4-st
rep

BEGIN CHART 3
Next row (WS) P1 work to rep line, work 14-st rep 6 times, p1 in last color used.
Next row (RS) K1, work 14-st rep 6 times, work to end of chart, k1 in last color used.
Cont to work chart in this manner until row 12 is complete.
With A, knit 1 row.

BEGIN CHART 4
Next row (RS) K1, work 4-st rep 24 times, work to end of chart, p1.
Cont to work chart in this manner until row 6 is complete. Break B.
Change to size 6 (4mm) needles.
Cont in St st with A only until piece measures 28"/71cm from beg, end with a WS row. Set panel aside.

Right Panel
Work as for left panel.

Finishing
Join panels using 3-needle bind-off method.

EDGING
With circular needle, A and RS facing, pick up and k 326 sts along one side edge. Work 14 rows in k2, p2 rib. Bind off. Rep for other side.

BUTTON AND BUTTON LOOP
Using photo as guide, sew button to left panel above Fair Isle band where the edging meets the panel. With crochet hook and A, chain 14, fasten off. Sew chain to edge of ribbing to correspond to button. ■

19

Fringed Handbag

Fringe lends a vintage vibe to a purse with a pretty allover
texture and practical zippered closure.

DESIGNED BY JACQUELINE VAN DILLEN

Knitted Measurements
Approx 11 x 9 x 1½"/28 x 23 x 4cm

Materials
■ 2 3½oz/100g hanks (each approx 219yd/200m) of Cascade Yarns *Venezia Worsted* (merino wool/mulberry silk) in #108 autumn walk

■ One pair each sizes 6 and 8 (4 and 5mm) needles *or size to obtain gauge*

■ One 12"/30cm non-separating zipper

■ 2 lengths of 5mm tubing, each 21"/54cm long, for handles

■ Sewing needle and thread to match yarn

■ Tapestry needle

■ Stitch markers

Plaited Basket Stitch
(over an odd number of sts)
Row 1 (RS) K2, *insert RH needle between next 2 sts from back to front, k the 2nd st, leaving it on the LH needle, k the first st, letting both sts drop from needle rep; from *, end k1.
Row 2 P2, *skip next st on LH needle and p the 2nd st, leaving on LH needle, p the first st and let both sts drop from needle; rep from *, end p1.
Rep rows 1 and 2 for plaited basket st.

Handbag
FRONT AND BACK (ONE PIECE)
With smaller needles, cast on 61 sts. Work in St st (k on RS, p on WS) for 7 rows.
Next (inc) row (WS) Purl, inc 20 sts evenly across—81 sts.
Change to larger needles. Work in plaited basket st until piece measures 20½"/52cm from beg, end with a WS row. Change to smaller needles.
Next (dec) row (RS) Knit, dec 20 sts evenly across—61 sts.
Work in St st for 7 rows more.

SIDE GUSSETS
Fold body of bag in half and place markers to mark center 1½"/4cm along each side. With smaller needles and RS facing, pick up and k 13 sts between markers on one side.
Next row (WS) K1, *p1, k1; rep from * to end for k1, p1 rib.
Next row K the knit sts and p the purl sts. Cont in rib until gusset is 1½"/4cm longer than side of bag. Bind off. Rep for

other side. Block piece if desired.

HANDLES (MAKE 2)
With smaller needles, cast on 6 sts. Work in St st until strip measures 22"/56cm from beg. Bind off. Place tube on knitted strip and sew sides closed around tube. Rep for 2nd handle.

Fringe
Cut 112 strands of yarn, each 7"/18cm long. With 2 strands and tapestry needle, beg at side edge and last row of plaited basket st on back of bag, thread strands from front to back between first 2 sts. Then bring yarn out from back to front on RH side of first st, then thread from front to back on LH side of 2nd st. Bring yarn to front between the 2 sts. Pull strand even. Rep 28 times across top of bag. Then rep for front of bag.

Finishing
Sew the sides of the gussets to the sides of the bag.
Fold the St st upper edges to WS and sew in place. Sew the handles in place, using photo as guide. Sew the zipper to the lower edge of the St st bands on front and back. Fold the side gusset ribbing to the WS and sew in place. ■

Gauges
20 sts and 28 rows to 4"/10cm over St st using larger needles.
26 sts and 20 rows over plaited basket st using smaller needles.
Take time to check gauges.

Mini Cable Collar

A menswear-inspired collar places crisp twisted-stitch cables against a background of seed and garter stitch.

DESIGNED BY ERICA SCHLUETER

◼◼◼▭

Knitted Measurements
Length 23"/58.5cm
Width 4½"/11.5

Materials
- 1 3½oz/100g hanks (each approx 307½yd/281m) of Cascade Yarns *Venezia Sport* (merino wool/mulberry silk) in #173 grey
- One pair size 5 (3.75mm) needles *or size to obtain gauge*
- Size E/4 (3.5mm) crochet hook
- One ⅝"/15mm button

Chain (or Crochet) Cast-On
1) Make a slip knot on the crochet hook. Hold the needle and yarn in your left hand with the yarn under the needle. Wrap the yarn around the hook for a crochet st. Pull the yarn through the hook.
2) Bring the yarn to the back under the needle, wrap the yarn for a crochet st and pull it through the loop on the hook. Rep this step until the desired number of sts has been cast on, minus one.
3) Sl the loop from the hook to the needle for the last cast-on st.

Collar
Cast on 27 sts using chain (or crochet) cast-on method.

BEGIN CHART
Row 1 (WS) Work chart pat over 27 sts. Cont to work chart in this manner until row 21 is complete.
Next (buttonhole) row (RS) Work chart row 22 to last 4 sts, bind off 2 sts, work to end of row.

Next row K2, cast on 2 sts, rep chart row 1 as established.
Cont in pat, rep rows 1–22, omitting buttonhole, until piece measures approx 23"/58.5cm from beg, end with a row 22. Bind off in pat.

Finishing
Sew on button 2"/5cm below bound-off edge and ½"/1.5cm in from edge that buttonhole is on. ◼

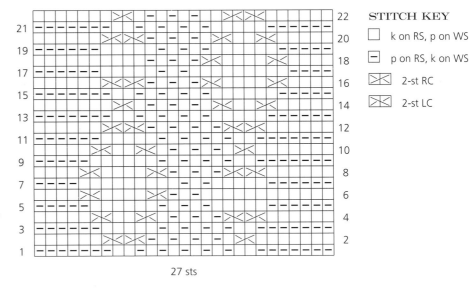

27 sts

STITCH KEY
- ☐ k on RS, p on WS
- ⊟ p on RS, k on WS
- ⧖ 2-st RC
- ⧗ 2-st LC

Gauge
24 sts and 34 rows to 4"/10cm over chart pat using size 5 (3.75mm) needles.
Take time to check gauge.

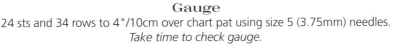

21

Lacy Layered Hat

An open lace pattern over a white underlayer evokes snowflakes
and adds an extra bit of warmth.

DESIGNED BY LISA SILVERMAN

Knitted Measurements
Brim circumference (unstretched)
16¾"/42.5cm
Height
7½"/19cm

Materials
■ 1 3½oz/100g hank (each approx 307½yd/281m) of Cascade Yarns *Venezia Sport* (merino wool/mulberry silk) each in #110 pure diamond (A) and #195 deep navy (B)

■ One each sizes 3 and 5 (3.25 and 3.75mm) circular needle, 16"/40cm long, *or size to obtain gauge*

■ One set (5) each sizes 3 and 5 (3.25 and 3.75mm) double-pointed needles (dpns)

■ Stitch marker

Lace Pattern
(multiple of 6 sts)
Rnd 1 *Yo, ssk, k1, k2tog, yo, k1; rep from * around.
Rnd 2 and all even-numbered rnds Knit.
Rnd 3 K1, *yo, k3; rep from * to last 2 sts, yo, k2.
Rnd 5 Sl 1 st purlwise, *yo, ssk, k1, k2tog, yo, sssk, rep from * to last 7 sts, yo, ssk, k1, k2tog, yo, sl 2 sts to RH needle, remove marker, sl sts back to LH needle, sssk, replace marker.
Rnd 7 *K2tog, yo, k1, yo, ssk, k1; rep from * around.
Rnd 9 Rep rnd 3.
Rnd 11 *K2tog, yo, sssk, yo, ssk, k1; rep from * around.
Rnd 12 Knit. Rep rnds 1–12 for lace pat.

Hat
UNDERLAYER
With smaller circular needle and A, cast on 108 sts. Place marker (pm) for beg of rnd and join, being careful not to twist sts.
Next rnd *K1, p1; rep from * around for k1, p1 rib.

Work in k1, p1 rib for 4 rnds more. Work in St st (k every rnd) until piece measures 6"/15cm from beg.

SHAPE CROWN
Note Change to smaller dpns when there are too few sts to fit comfortably on circular needle.
Rnd 1 [K7, k2tog] 12 times around—96 sts.
Rnds 2, 4, 6, 8, and 10 Knit.
Rnd 3 [K6, k2tog] 12 times around—84 sts.
Rnd 5 [K5, k2tog] 12 times around—72 sts.
Rnd 7 [K4, k2tog] 12 times around—60 sts.
Rnd 9 [K3, k2tog] 12 times around—48 sts.
Rnd 11 [K2, k2tog] 12 times around—36 sts.
Rnd 12 [K1, k2tog] 12 times around—24 sts.

Gauges
26 sts and 41 rnds to 4"/10cm over St st using smaller needles.
15 sts and 29 rnds to 4"/10cm over lace pat using larger needles.
Take time to check gauges.

Lacy Layered Hat

Rnds 13 and 14 *K2tog; rep from * around—6 sts.
Break yarn, leaving a long tail. Thread through open sts and pull tightly to close.

LACE LAYER
With larger circular needle, RS facing, and A, working in first row above ribbing, pick up and k 72 sts evenly around entire underlayer. Break A. Join B and pm for beg of rnd. Knit 2 rnds.

BEGIN LACE PAT
Work rnds 1–12 of lace pat 3 times, then rep rnds 1 and 2 once more.

SHAPE CROWN
Note Change to larger dpns when there are too few sts to fit comfortably on circular needle.
Rnd 1 K1, *yo, sssk, yo, k3, rep from * to last 5 sts, yo, sssk, yo, k2.
Rnds 2, 4, 6, and 8 Knit.
Rnd 3 *K1, k2tog, yo, sssk, yo, ssk; rep from * to end of rnd—54 sts.
Rnd 5 *K2, ssk, k2tog; rep from * to end of rnd—36 sts.
Rnd 7 Sl 1 purlwise, *ssk, k2tog; rep from * to last 3 sts, ssk, remove marker and k last st of rnd tog with 1st st of next rnd—18 sts.
Rnd 9 [Sssk, k3tog] 3 times around—6 sts.
Break yarn, leaving a long tail. Thread tail through open sts and pull tightly to close. Then thread tail through center top of both layers, to tack in place. ■

Quick Tip
Be sure to make gauge swatches for both the Stockinette stitch and the lace layers. And don't forget to block those swatches!

Lace Kerchief

A jaunty pull-through kerchief with a simple leaf motif at each end keeps the chill at bay in style.

DESIGNED BY COURTNEY CEDARHOLM

Knitted Measurements
Width
approx 8½"/21.5cm
Length
approx 29"/73.5cm

Materials
■ 1 3½oz/100g hank (each approx 219yd/200m) of Cascade Yarns *Venezia Worsted* (merino wool/mulberry silk) in #161 turquoise

■ One pair size 7 (4.5mm) needles *or size to obtain gauge*

■ Two size 7 (4.5mm) double-pointed needles (dpns) for I-cord loop

■ Scrap yarn and crochet hook for provisional cast-on

■ Stitch markers

Provisional Cast on
Using scrap yarn and crochet hook, chain the number of sts to cast on, plus a few extra. Cut a tail and pull the tail through the last chain. With knitting needle and yarn, pick up and knit the stated number of sts through the "purl bumps" on the back of the chain. To remove scrap chain, when instructed, pull out the tail from the last crochet st. Gently and slowly pull on the tail to unravel the crochet sts, carefully placing each released knit st on a needle.

Kerchief
I-CORD LOOP
With 2 dpns, cast on 6 sts using provisional cast-on method.
*Knit one row. Without turning work, slide the sts back to the opposite end of needle to work next row from RS. Pull yarn tightly from the end of the row. Rep from * until I-cord measures 7"/18cm from beg.
Next (joining) row (RS) Carefully undo scrap yarn and place 6 live sts on dpn with rem 6 sts, being careful not to twist I-cord loop, k12. Turn to beg working back and forth in rows.
Change to straight needles.
Work 3 rows in St st.

SHAPE END
Next row (RS) K6, yo, k2tog, k to end.
Next and all WS rows Purl.
Next (set-up) row K6, place marker (pm), yo, k1, pm, yo, k to end—14 sts.
Purl 1 row.

Gauge
21 sts and 30 rows to 4"/10cm over St st using size 7 (4.5mm) needles.
Take time to check gauge.

22 Lace Kerchief

STITCH KEY

- ☐ k on RS, p on WS
- ☑ k2tog
- ☒ SKP
- ⊡ yo

beg with 36 sts

Next (inc) row (RS) [K to marker, sl marker, yo] twice, k to end—2 sts inc'd. Rep inc row every other row 6 times more—28 sts.
Purl 1 row.
Next row (RS) K14, yo, k2tog, k to end.
Purl 1 row.
Next (set-up) row (RS) K14, pm, yo, k1, yo, pm, k to end—30 sts.
Purl 1 row.
Next (inc) row (RS) [K to marker, sl marker, yo] twice, k to end—2 sts inc'd. Rep inc row every other row 7 times more—46 sts.
Work even in St st until piece measures

15"/38cm from joining row, end with a WS row.

Next (dec) row (RS) K2, SKP, k to last 4 sts, k2tog, k2—2 sts dec'd. Rep dec row every 8th row 5 times more—34 sts.

BEGIN CHART
Work rows 1–34 of chart pat—6 sts.
Next (dec) row (RS) [K2tog] 3 times.
Next row P3tog. Fasten off.

FINISHING
Block to open lace. ∎

Fair Isle Arm Warmers

The perfect winter accessory: long ribs keep your arms toasty while a gorgeous Fair Isle pattern peeks out of your coat sleeves.

DESIGNED BY YOKO HATTA

■■■□

Knitted Measurements
Hand circumference
7½"/19cm
Length
11½"/29cm

Materials
■ 1 3½oz/100g hank (each approx 307½yd/281m) of Cascade Yarns *Venezia Sport* (merino wool/mulberry silk) in #173 grey (A)

■ Small amount each in #187 sage (B), #194 cranberry (C), #197 spring green (D), #196 lagoon (bright blue, E), #193 power pink (F), and #179 deep sea (dark blue, G)

■ One set (4) each sizes 3 and 4 (3.25 and 3.5mm) double-pointed needles (dpns) *or size to obtain gauge*

■ Scrap yarn

■ Stitch markers

K2, P1 Rib
(multiple of 3 sts)
Rnd 1 *K2, p1; rep from * around.
Rep rnd 1 for k2, p1 rib.

Left Arm Warmer
With smaller needles and A, cast on 48 sts and divide on 3 dpns. Place marker (pm) for beg of rnd and join, being careful not to twist sts.
Work in k2, p1 rib until piece measures 5½"/14cm from beg.
Change to larger needles. Knit 2 rnds A.

BEGIN CHART 1
Rnd 1 Work 6-st rep 8 times around.
Cont to work chart in this manner until rnd 10 is complete.

BEGIN CHART 2
Next rnd Work 16-st rep 3 times around.
Cont to work chart in this manner until rnd 15 is complete.

AFTERTHOUGHT THUMB SET-UP
Next rnd With A, k to last 7 sts; with scrap yarn, k7, slip scrap yarn sts back to LH needle and knit them again with A.

Knit 1 rnd A.
Rep rnds 1–10 of chart 1 once more.
Change to smaller needles.
Work 8 rnds in k2, p1 rib. Bind off.

THUMB
Carefully remove scrap yarn, placing sts from upper edge of thumb opening on 1 dpn, and sts from lower edge of thumb opening on a 2nd dpn.
Next rnd With A and smaller dpns, beg with lower edge sts, k7, pick up and k 2 sts, k upper edge sts, pick up and k 1 st, pm for beg of rnd—17 sts.
Work 8 rnds in St st. Bind off.

Right Arm Warmer
Work as for left arm warmer to afterthought thumb set-up.
Next rnd With scrap yarn, k7, place scrap yarn sts back on LH needle and knit them again with A.
Cont and complete as for left arm warmer. ■

Gauge
25 sts and 29 rnds to 4"/10cm over chart pats using larger needles.
Take time to check gauge.

Fair Isle Arm Warmers

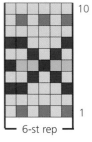

CHART 1

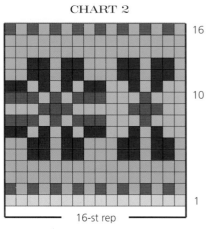

10

1

6-st rep

CHART 2

16

10

1

16-st rep

COLOR KEY

- Grey (A)
- Sage (B)
- Cranberry (C)
- Spring green (D)
- Lagoon (E)
- Power pink (F)
- Deep sea (G)

Cabled Headband

Cables emphasize the graceful shaping of a
headband with I-cord edging and ties.

DESIGNED BY SUE MINK AND NATALIE DERSE

Knitted Measurements

Width at widest point
4½"/11.5 cm
Length excluding ties
16"/40.5cm

Materials

■ 1 3½oz/100g hank (each approx
307½yd/281m) of Cascade Yarns
Venezia Sport (merino wool/mulberry silk)
in #196 lagoon

■ One pair size 4 (3.5mm) needles
or size to obtain gauge

■ Two size 4 (3.5mm)
double-pointed needles (dpns)

■ Cable needle (cn)

Stitch Glossary

3-st RPC Sl next st to cn and hold to
back, k2, p1 from cn.
3-st LPC Sl 2 sts to cn and hold to *front*,
p1, k2 from cn.
4-st RC Sl 2 sts to cn and hold to *back*,
k2, k2 from cn.
4-st LC Sl 2 sts to cn and hold to *front*,
k2, k2 from cn.
4-st RPC Sl 2 sts to cn and hold to *back*,
k2, p2 from cn.
4-st LPC Sl 2 sts to cn and hold to *front*,
p2, k2 from cn.

Headband

FIRST I-CORD TIE

With 2 dpns, cast on 5 sts. *Knit one
row. Without turning work, slide sts back
to the opposite end of needle to work
next row from RS. Pull yarn tightly from
end of row. Rep from * until I-cord
measures 8"/20.5cm from beg.

BEGIN CHART 1

Change to straight needles to work row
1 of chart 1. When row 1 is complete,
turn to work row 2 on WS.
Cont to foll chart 1 through row
40—28 sts.

BEGIN CHART 2

Cont to foll chart until row 74 is
complete. Rep rows 55–70 once more.
Cont with row 93 of chart 2 and work
until row 104 is complete.

BEGIN CHART 3

Cont to foll chart 3 until row 142 is
complete—5 sts.

Gauge

28 sts and 36 rows to 4"/10cm over chart 2 pat using size 4 (3.5mm) needles.
Take time to check gauge.

Cabled Headband

CHART 1

28 sts

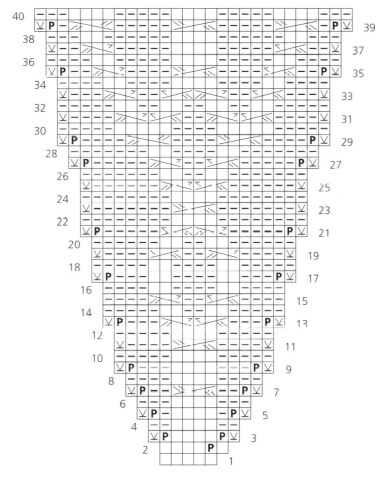

SECOND I-CORD TIE
Change to dpns to work I-cord as for first
I-cord tie.
When 2nd tie measures same as first tie,
bind off.

Finishing
I-CORD EDGING
Note Work into sl sts along headband
edge to pick up and k the sts for
applied I-cord. Be sure to pick up 1 st
where I-cord tie meets body of headband
at each end.
With dpn, cast on 4 sts. *K3, pick up and
k 1 st along edge of headband and knit it
tog with last st on dpn. Without turning
work, slide sts back to opposite end of
needle to work next row on RS.
Pull yarn tightly from end of row. Rep
from * until all sts along one side edge
have been worked. Bind off rem sts.
Rep for other side. ■

STITCH KEY

☐ k on RS, p on WS	3-st LPC
─ p on RS, k on WS	4-st RC
⋁ slip 1 wyib	4 st LC
P M1 p-st	4-st RPC
◿ p2 tog	4-st LPC
3-st RPC	

Cabled Headband

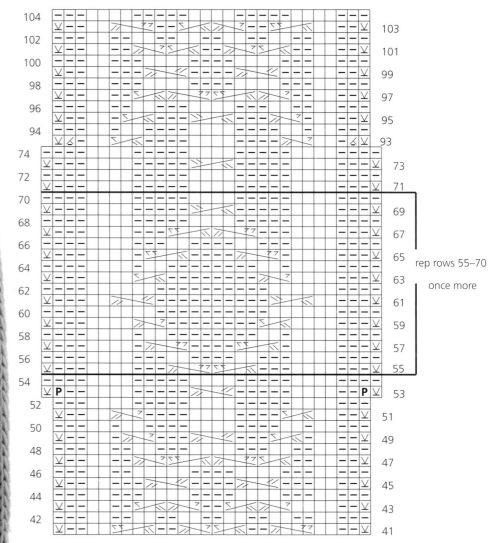

CHART 2

rep rows 55–70

once more

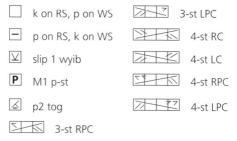

24 Cabled Headband

CHART 3

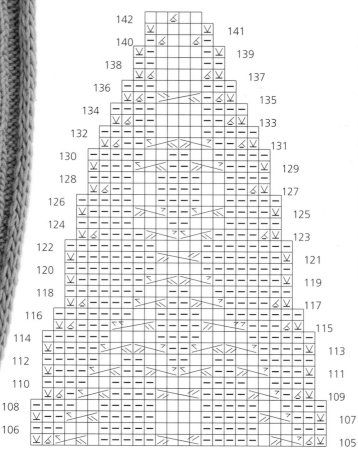

STITCH KEY

☐	k on RS, p on WS		⊼⊼	3-st LPC
─	p on RS, k on WS		⊼⊼	4-st RC
⋁	slip 1 wyib		⊼⊼	4-st LC
P	M1 p-st		⊼⊼	4-st RPC
⊿	p2 tog		⊼⊼	4-st LPC
⊼⊼	3-st RPC			

Lace and Cable Shawl

Geometric shaping combined with bands of lace and a cabled edging creates a balance of structure and femininity.

DESIGNED BY ERICA SCHLUETER

Knitted Measurements

Width along cable edge
51"/130cm
Length
12"/31cm

Materials

- 3 3½oz/100g hanks (each approx 219yd/200m) of Cascade Yarns *Venezia Worsted* (merino wool/mulberry silk) in #178 deep sea
- One pair size 8 (5mm) needles *or size to obtain gauge*
- Cable needle (cn)

Stitch Glossary

12-st LC Sl 6 sts to cn and hold to *front*, work 6 sts in rib, work 6 sts from cn in rib.

ssk Sl 1 knitwise to LH needle, sl next st purlwise to RH needle, insert LH needle into the fronts of the 2 sl sts and k them tog.

K1, P1 Rib

(over an even number of sts)
Row 1 *K1, p1; rep from * to end.
Row 2 K the knit sts and p the purl sts
Rep row 2 for k1, p1 rib.

Lace Pattern

(multiple of 7 sts)
Row 1 (WS) *P2, yo, ssk, k1, k2tog, yo; rep from * to end.
Row 2 *P5, k2; rep from * to end.
Row 3 *P2, k1, yo, SK2P, yo, k1; rep from * to end.
Row 4 Rep row 2.
Rep rows 1–4 for lace pat.

Cable Pattern

(over 12 sts)
Row 1 (WS) *K1, p1; rep from * to end.
Rows 2–9 K the knit sts and p the purl sts.
Row 10 (RS) 12-st LC. Rep rows 1–10 for cable pat.

Gauge

18 sts and 24 rows to 4"/10cm over St st using size 8 (5mm) needles.
Take time to check gauge.

Lace and Cable Shawl

Notes

1) Shawl is worked from side to side.
2) Shawl can be worn with either side public.

Shawl

Cast on 12 sts. Work rows 1–8 of cable pat.

Next row (WS) Cast on 9 sts, work row 1 of lace pat over 7 sts, place marker (pm), p2, work cable pat to end.

Next (cable) row (RS) Work row 10 of cable pat, k2, sl marker, work row 2 of lace pat. Cont to work pats in this manner, sl marker every row, until row 4 of lace pat is complete, then rep rows 1–4 once more. AT THE SAME TIME, cont to rep rows 1–10 of cable pat as established.

*Next row (WS) Cast on 7 sts, work lace pat to marker, sl marker, p2, work cable pat to end.

Cont in pats as established for 7 rows more; rep from * 3 times more.

Next row (WS) Cast on 7 sts, work lace pat to marker, sl marker, work cable pat to end—56 sts. Place yarn marker at end of row. Cont in pats as established until row 4 of lace pat has been completed 19 times from yarn marker. Remove yarn marker and place new yarn marker at end of row just worked.

Next row (WS) Cast on 7 sts, work lace pat to marker, sl marker, work cable pat to end—63 sts.

Cont in pats as established until row 4 of lace pat has been completed 17 times from yarn marker. Remove yarn marker and place new yarn marker at end of row just worked.

Next row (WS) Bind off 7 sts, work in pats to end—56 sts. Cont in pats as established until row 4 of lace pat has been completed 19 times from yarn marker.

*Next row (WS) Bind off 7 sts, work lace pat to marker, sl marker, p2, work cable pat to end. Cont in pats as established for 7 rows more; rep from * 4 times more—21 sts.

Next row (WS) Bind off 9 sts, work cable pat to end. Work 9 rows more in k1, p1 rib. Bind off rem 12 sts. ■

26 Daisy Chain Fringe Scarf

A floral lace motif on wide bands brings fringe to the forefront of a stockinette scarf.

DESIGNED BY CAROLYN NOYES

Knitted Measurements
Width approx 10¾"/27.5cm
Length approx 78"/198cm

Materials
■ 3 3½oz/100g hanks (each approx 307½yd/281m) of Cascade Yarns *Venezia Sport* (merino wool/mulberry silk) in #132 mouse

■ One pair size 7 (4.5mm) needles *or size to obtain gauge*

Daisy Chain Stitch
(multiple of 6 sts plus 1)
Row 1 (WS) Knit.
Row 2 K1, *k5, wrapping yarn 3 times for each st, k1; rep from * to end.
Row 3 *K1, [sl next st wyif, dropping extra wraps] 5 times, [bring yarn to back between needles and sl the 5 sts back to LH needle, bring yarn to front between needles and sl the 5 sts to RH needle] twice, k1; rep from * to last st, k1.
Rows 4 and 5 Knit.
Work rows 1–5 for daisy chain st.

Scarf
Cast on 57 sts. Knit 1 row.
Next row (RS) K1, sl 1, k to last 2 sts, sl 1, k1.
Next row Purl.
Rep last 2 rows until piece measures 78"/198cm from beg, end with a RS row.
Next row Knit.
Bind off.

FRINGE (MAKE 10)
Cast on 37 sts. Work rows 1–5 of daisy chain st. Bind off as foll:
Bind off 1 st, *bind off 4, k2tog and bind off resulting st; rep from * to last 5 sts, bind off 3 sts, k2tog and bind off rem st.

Finishing
Sew 5 pieces of fringe to each end, lining up first and last pieces with side edges and leaving 8 sts between each piece. ■

Gauge
21 sts and 28 rows to 4"/10cm over St st using size 7 (4.5mm) needles.
Take time to check gauge.

27

Geometric Mitts

Corrugated ribbing and a diamond colorwork motif get dimension
from a blend of solid and variegated yarns.

DESIGNED BY CHERYL MURRAY

Size
Woman's Small/Medium

Knitted Measurements
Hand circumference 7½"/19cm
Length 8"/20.5cm

Materials
■ 1 3½oz/100g hank (each approx
307½yd/281m) of Cascade Yarns
Venezia Sport (merino wool/mulberry silk)
in #160 ginger (A)

■ 1 3½oz/100g hank (each approx
307½yd/281m) of Cascade Yarns *Venezia
Sport Multis* (merino wool/mulberry silk)
in #208 citrus cream (B)

■ One set (5) size 3 (3.25mm)
double-pointed needles (dpns)
or size to obtain gauge

■ Scrap yarn

■ Stitch markers

Corrugated Rib
(multiple of 4 sts)
Rnd 1 *K2 with A, p2 with B; rep from *
around.
Rep rnd 1 for corrugated rib.

Left Mitt
CUFF
With A, cast on 60 sts. Place marker (pm)
for beg of rnd and join, being careful not
to twist sts.
Next rnd *K2 with A, k2 with B; rep from
* around.

BEGIN CORRUGATED RIB
Work in corrugated rib until cuff measures
3"/7.5cm from beg.

BEGIN CHART PAT
Rnd 1 Work 12-st rep 5 times around.
Cont to work chart in this manner until rnd
12 is complete. Rep rnds 1–12 once more.

PLACE THUMB
Next rnd Work rnd 1 of chart to last 12
sts; with scrap yarn, k next 10 sts, place
10 scrap yarn sts back on LH needle and
work rnd 1 of chart to end of rnd.
Cont to work in chart pat until rnd 12
is complete.
Work in corrugated rib for 1"/2.5cm.
Bind off loosely with A.

THUMB
Carefully remove scrap yarn and place 10
sts from below the opening on 1 dpn,
place 10 sts above the opening on a 2nd
dpn—20 sts. Divide sts evenly on dpns.

Next rnd *K2 with
A, k2 with B; rep
from * around.
Rep last rnd until
thumb measures
1"/2.5cm. Bind off
loosely with A.

Right Mitt
Work as for left mitt to Place Thumb.

PLACE THUMB
Next rnd Work first 2 sts of rnd 1 of
chart; with scrap yarn, k next 10 sts, place
10 scrap yarn sts back on LH needle and
work rnd 1 of chart to end of rnd.
Complete as for left mitt. ■

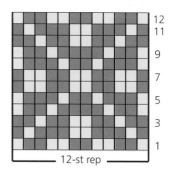

└ 12-st rep ┘

COLOR KEY

■ Ginger (A) □ Citrus cream (B)

Soutache Capelet

A picot edging and soutache-inspired I-cord trim embellish an easy stockinette stitch wrap.

DESIGNED BY JEAN SUZUKI

Knitted Measurements
Width along lower edge
59"/150cm
Width along upper edge
29"/73.5cm
Length
13"/33cm

Materials
- 3 3½oz/100g hanks (each approx 219yd/200m) of Cascade Yarns *Venezia Worsted* (merino wool/mulberry silk) in #132 mouse (A)
- 1 3½oz/100g hank (each approx 307½yd/281m) of Cascade Yarns *Venezia Sport* (merino wool/mulberry silk) in #132 mouse (B) for I-cord trim
- One each sizes 4 and 6 (3.5 and 4mm) circular needle *or size to obtain gauge*
- Two size 2 (2.75mm) double-pointed needles (dpns) for I-cord trim
- Size E/4 (3.5mm) crochet hook
- Two 1"/25mm buttons
- Stitch markers
- Safety pins

Notes
1) Capelet is worked from the top down in rows. Circular needle is used to accommodate large number of sts. Do not join.
2) Capelet is asymmetric. The front left panel corresponds to the panel that is worn over the right shoulder.

Capelet
PICOT NECKLINE
With smaller circular needle and A, cast on 104 sts.
Work 4 rows in St st.
Next (picot) row (RS) K2, *k2tog, yo; rep from * to last 2 sts, k2.
Work 5 rows in St st.

Gauge
18 sts and 26 rows to 4"/10cm over St st using larger needle and A.
Take time to check gauge.

Soutache Capelet

Change to larger needles for body.
Work in St st for 2 rows.
Next row (RS) K18, place marker (pm),
[k17, pm] twice, k18, pm, k17, pm, k17.
Next row Purl, slipping markers.
Next (inc) row (RS) [K1, M1, k to 1 st
before marker M1, k1, sl marker] 5 times,
M1, k to the last st, M1, k1—12 sts inc'd.
Next row (WS) Purl.
Rep inc row every other row 8
times more, then every 4th row
3 times—248 sts.
Work even in St st until piece measures
13"/33cm from picot row, end with
a WS row.
Next row (RS) Rep picot row.
Change to smaller circular needle. Work
5 rows in St st. Bind off.

Finishing
Block to measurements.
Fold neck edge along picot row to WS.
Pin, then whipstitch in place. Rep for
lower edge.

LEFT FRONT EDGE
With RS facing, crochet hook and A,
join with sl st at neck edge, ch 1,
*sc in each of next 2 sts, skip 1 st, sc in
next st; rep from * along entire
edge to bottom of picot hem.
Next 2 rows Ch 1, sc in each sc across.
Fasten off.

RIGHT FRONT EDGE
With RS facing, crochet hook and A,
join with sl st at hem edge, ch 1, *sc in
each of next 2 sts, skip 1 st, sc in next st;
rep from * along entire edge to top of
picot edge.
Next row (WS) Ch 1, sc in each sc.
Place a marker 3"/7.5cm down from
picot neck edge.
Next (button loop) row (RS) Ch 1,
sc in each sc to marker, ch 4, skip 3 sc,
sc in next 2 sc, ch 4, skip 3 sc, sc in
each sc to end.

BUTTON LOOPS
Join with sl st to base of first button loop,
sc in each ch, sl st in next sc, fasten off.
Rep for 2nd button loop.

I-CORD TRIM
With 2 dpns and B, cast on 3 sts.
*Knit one row. Without turning work,
slide the sts back to the opposite end of
needle to work next row from RS. Pull
yarn tightly from the end of the row.
Rep from * until I-cord measures approx
153"/389cm. Place I-cord sts on a safety
pin to hold. Do not break yarn.
Lay capelet flat. Using photo as guide,
beg at hem edge, form loops and swirls
along entire edge of capelet, working
around neck edge and down to opposite
side of hem, pinning loops to capelet
as you go. Adjust length of I-cord and
bind off.
With B and tapestry needle, sew I-cord
to capelet.
Sew buttons to correspond to
button loops. ∎

Leafy Lace & Cable Cowl

A lacy leaf motif that incorporates cables makes a cowl
that's both delicate and substantial.

DESIGNED BY E. J. SLAYTON

■■■▢

Knitted Measurements
Circumference at lower edge
approx 26"/66cm
Height
11"/28cm

Materials
■ 1 3½oz/100g hank (each approx
307½yd/281m) of Cascade Yarns
Venezia Sport (merino wool/mulberry silk)
in #130 denim

■ Size 4 (3.5mm) circular needle,
16"/40cm long, *or size to obtain gauge*

■ Size 5 (3.75mm) circular needle,
24"/60cm long

■ Cable needle (cn)

■ Stitch marker

Stitch Glossary
6-st RC Sl 3 sts to cn and hold to *back*,
k3, k3 from cn.
6-st LC Sl 3 sts to cn and hold to *front*,
k3, k3 from cn.

Cowl
With larger needle, cast on 144 sts.
Place marker (pm) and join, being careful
not to twist sts.
[Purl 1 rnd, knit 1 rnd] twice.

BEGIN CHART 1
Rnd 1 Work 16-st rep of chart 1 nine
times around.
Cont to work chart 1 in this manner
until rnd 6 is complete. Rep rnds 1–6
once more.

BEGIN CHART 2
Next rnd Work 16-st rep of chart 2 nine
times around.
Cont to work chart 2 in this manner
until rnd 10 is complete. Rep rnds 1–8
once more.
Next (dec) rnd [P1, k3tog, k2, yo, k1, yo,
p1, yo, k1, yo, k2, sssk, p2tog] 9 times
around—135 sts.
Next rnd Beg with rnd 2, work 15-st rep
of chart 1 nine times around.

Gauge
25 sts and 28 rnds to 4"/10cm after blocking over charts 1 and 2 using smaller needles.
Take time to check gauge.

Leafy Lace & Cable Cowl

CHART 1

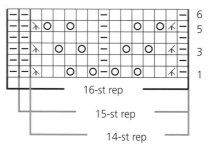

16-st rep

15-st rep

14-st rep

CHART 2

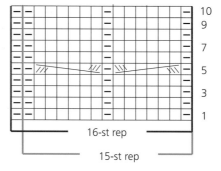

16-st rep

15-st rep

STITCH KEY

☐ k on RS, p on WS

— p on RS, k on WS

Ⓞ yo

k3tog

sssk

6-st RC

6-st LC

Cont to work chart 1 in this manner until rnd 6 is complete. Work rnds 1–6 of chart 1 once more.

Next rnd Beg with rnd 1, work 15–st rep of chart 2 nine times around.

Cont to work chart 2 in this manner until rnd 4 is complete.

Change to smaller needles.

Cont to work chart 2 until rnd 10 is complete, then rep rnds 1–8 once more.

Next (dec) rnd P1, [k3tog, k2, yo, k1, yo, p1, yo, k1, yo, k2, sssk, p2tog] 8 times, work in pat to last st, pm for new beg of rnd, p last st tog with first st of next rnd—126 sts.

Next rnd Work 14-st rep of chart 1, rnd 2 for 9 times around.

Cont to work chart 1 in this manner until rnd 6 is complete. Work rnds 1–6 of chart 1 once more.

Purl 1 rnd.

Bind off loosely purlwise. ■

30

Catalpa Hat

A cable pattern inspired by catalpa leaves is the perfect complement to a variegated colorway of forest tones.

DESIGNED BY ANASTASIA BLAES

Knitted Measurements
Circumference at brim (unstretched)
15½"/39.5cm
Length
7¾"/19.5cm

Materials
■ 1 3½oz/100g hank (each approx 307½yd/281m) of Cascade Yarns *Venezia Sport Multis* (merino wool/mulberry silk) in #204 greens
■ One set (5) each sizes 4 and 5 (3.5 and 3.75mm) double-pointed needles (dpns) *or size to obtain gauge*
■ Stitch marker

Note
The stitch count of the lace pat changes from row to row.

Hat
BRIM
With smaller needles, cast on 120 sts. Divide evenly on 4 dpns. Place marker (pm) for beg of rnd and join, being careful not to twist sts.
Next rnd *P2, k1, rep from * around for rib pat.
Work in rib pat until brim measures 1½"/4cm from beg.
Change to larger needles.

BEGIN LEAF PAT
Rnd 1 *P2, yo, k1, yo, p2, k2, k2tog, k3; rep from * around—130 sts.
Rnd 2 *P2, k3, p2, k6; rep from * around.
Rnd 3 *P2, k1, [yo, k1] twice, p2, k2, k2tog, k2; rep from * around—140 sts.
Rnd 4 *P2, k5, rep from * around.
Rnd 5 *P2, k2, yo, k1, yo, k2, p2, k2, k2tog, k1, rep from * around—150 sts.
Rnd 6 *P2, k7, p2, k4; rep from * around.
Rnd 7 *P2, k3, yo, k1, yo, k3, p2, k2, k2tog, rep from * around—160 sts.
Rnd 8 *P2, k9, p2, k3, rep from * around.
Rnd 9 *P2, k2, k2tog, k5, p2, k1, k2tog, rep from * around—140 sts.
Rnd 10 *P2, k8, p2, k2; rep from * around.
Rnd 11 *P2, k2, k2tog, k4, p2, k2tog; rep from * around—120 sts.
Rnd 12 *P2, k7, p2, k1; rep from * around.
Rnd 13 *P2, k2, k2tog, k3, p2, yo, k1, yo; rep from * around—130 sts.
Rnd 14 *P2, k6, p2, k3; rep from * around.

Gauge
22 sts and 32 rows to 4"/10cm after blocking over St st using larger needles.
Take time to check gauge.

Catalpa Hat

Rnd 15 *P2, k2, k2tog, k2, p2, k1, [yo, k1] twice; rep from * around—140 sts.

Rnd 16 *P2, k5; rep from * around.

Rnd 17 *P2, k2, k2tog, k1, p2, k2, yo, k1, yo, k2; rep from * around—150 sts.

Rnd 18 *P2, k4, p2, k7; rep from * around.

Rnd 19 *P2, k2, k2tog, p2, k3, yo, k1, yo, k3; rep from * around—160 sts.

Rnd 20 *P2, k3, p2, k9; rep from * around.

Rnd 21 *P2, k1, k2tog, p2, k2, k2tog, k5; rep from * around—140 sts.

Rnd 22 *P2, k2, p2, k8; rep from * around.

Rnd 23 *P2, k2tog, p2, k2, k2tog, k4; rep from * around—120 sts.

Rnd 24 *P2, k1, p2, k7; rep from * around.

Rnds 25–36 Rep rnds 1–12.

CROWN SHAPING

Rnd 37 *P2, k2, k2tog, k3, p2, k1; rep from * around—110 sts.

Rnd 38 *P2, k6, p2, k1, rep from * around.

Rnd 39 *P2, k2, k2tog, k2, p2, k1; rep from * around—100 sts.

Rnd 40 *P2, k5, p2, k1; rep from * around.

Rnd 41 *P2, k2, k2tog, k1, p2, k1; rep from * around—90 sts.

Rnd 42 *P2, k4, p2, k1; rep from * around.

Rnd 43 *P2, k2, k2tog, p2, k1; rep from * around—80 sts.

Rnd 44 *P2, k3, p2, k1, rep from * around.

Rnd 45 *P2, k1, k2tog, p2, k1; rep from * around—70 sts.

Rnd 46 *P2, k2, p2, k1; rep from * around.

Rnd 47 *P2, k2tog, p2, k1; rep from * around—60 sts.

Rnd 48 *P2, k1; rep from * around.

Rnd 49 *P2, k1, p1, k2tog; rep from * around—50 sts.

Rnd 50 *P2, k1, p1, k1; rep from * around.

Rnd 51 *P2, k1, k2tog; rep from * around—40 sts.

Rnd 52 *P2, k2; rep from * around.

Rnd 53 P1, *ssk, k2tog, rep from * around to last 3 sts, end ssk, knit last st tog with first st of rnd—20 sts.

Rnd 54 [K2tog] 10 times around—10 sts. Break yarn and thread through rem sts. Pull tight to close. ■

Short Row Ruffled Shawl

A lacy ruffle and simple top edging are elegant finishing
touches on a beautifully draped shawl.

DESIGNED BY GRACE AKHREM

Knitted Measurements
**Width along upper edge
(not including ruffle)**
32"/81cm
**Length at center
(not including ruffle)**
15"/38cm

Materials
■ 2 3½oz/100g hanks (each approx
307½yd/281m) of Cascade Yarns
Venezia Sport (merino wool/mulberry silk)
in #178 deep sea foam (MC)

■ 1 hank in #168 blue spruce (CC)

■ One pair size 6 (4mm) needles
or size to obtain gauge

■ Size 6 (4mm) circular needle,
32"/80cm long

Short Row Wrap and Turn (w&t)
Knit (purl) side
1) Wyib, sl next st purlwise.
2) Move yarn between needles to front
(back).
3) Sl same st back to LH needle. Turn
work, bring yarn to knit (purl) side
between needles. One st is wrapped.
4) When short rows are completed, hide
all wraps as foll: work to just before
wrapped st. For knit side: Insert RH
needle under the wrap and knitwise into
the wrapped st, k them together. For purl
side: Insert RH needle from behind
into the back loop of the wrap and place
it on the LH needle; p wrap tog with st
on needle.

Short Row Pattern
Short row 1 (RS) Sl 1, k to last 3 sts,
w&t, k to end.
Short row 2 (RS) Sl 1, k to 3 sts before
previously wrapped st, w&t, k to end.
Rep short row 2 twenty times more.
Short row 23 (RS) Sl 1, w&t, k1.
Row 24 (RS) Sl 1, k to end, hiding all
wraps.
Row 25 (WS) Sl 1, k to end.
Rep rows 1–25 for short row pat.

Note Sl first st of every row wyif,
bring yarn to back between needles to
k the next st.

Shawl
With straight needles and MC,
cast on 70 sts.
Next 2 rows Sl 1, k to end.

Gauge
19 sts and 40 rows to 4"/10cm over garter st before blocking using size 6 (4mm) needles.
Take time to check gauge.

Short Row Ruffled Shawl

BEGIN SHORT ROW PAT
Work rows 1–25 of short row
pat 10 times.
Next row (RS) Sl 1, k to end.
Do not turn.

BACK NECK
Pick up and k 12 sts along center curve.
Next short row Sl 1, k11, w&t.
Next short row K9, w&t.
Next short row K6, w&t.
Next short row K to end, hiding
all wraps.
Bind off knitwise, hiding rem wraps.

Finishing
RUFFLE
With WS facing and CC, pick up and k
242 sts along slip st edge.
Row 1 (RS) Knit.
Row 2 and all WS rows Purl.
Row 3 K1, *yo, k5; rep from * to last st,
yo, k1.
Row 5 K1, *yo, k1, yo, k5; rep from * to
last 2 sts, yo, k1, yo, k1.
Row 7 K2, *yo, k1, yo, k3, [k1, yo, k1] in
next st, k3; rep from * to last 3 sts, yo,
k1, yo, k2.
Row 9 K3, *yo, k1, yo, k5, [k1, yo, k1] in
next st, k5; rep from * to last 4 sts, yo,
k1, yo, k3.
Row 10 Purl.
Bind off all sts, but do not fasten
off last st.

TOP EDGING
With rem CC loop on needle,
pick up and k 7 sts along ruffle edge,
152 sts along upper edge of shawl, and
8 sts along ruffle edge—168 sts.
Bind off knitwise. ∎

Cable and Bobble Leg Warmers

Cables twist around bobbles to form columns, while ribbing
lengthens the leg and makes for a snug fit.

DESIGNED BY JULIE GADDY

Knitted Measurements
**Calf circumference
(unstretched)**
10½"/26.5cm
Length
14½"/37cm

Materials
■ 2 3½oz/100g hanks (each approx
307½yd/281m) of Cascade Yarns
Venezia Sport (merino wool/mulberry silk)
in #173 grey
■ One pair size 5 (3.75mm) needles *or
size to obtain gauge*
■ Size 5 (3.75mm) circular needle,
16"/40cm long
■ Cable needle (cn)
■ Stitch marker

Stitch Glossary
Kfb Knit in front and back of st—1 st
increased.
M1 p-st Insert LH needle from front to
back under the strand between last st
worked and the next st on LH needle.
Purl into the back loop to twist the st—
1 st increased.

Make bobble (MB) K1, p1, k1 in same st,
making 3 sts from one; turn. P3, turn.
K3, turn. P3, turn. K3tog.
4-st RC Sl 2 sts to cn and hold to *back*,
k2, k2 from cn.
4-st LC Sl 2 sts to cn and hold to *front*,
k2, k2 from cn.

Notes
Leg warmers are worked back and forth
in rows from ankle to beg of top cuff. Sts
are joined in the rnd to knit cuff and then
leg is seamed.

Leg Warmers
LOWER CUFF
With straight needles, cast on 61 sts.
Next row (WS) P1, *k1, p1; rep from *
to end.
Next row (RS) K the knit sts and p the
purl sts for k1, p1 rib.
Work in k1, p1 rib until cuff measures
2"/5cm from beg, end with a RS row.

Gauges
35 sts and 34 rows to 4"/10cm over k1, p1 rib unstretched using size 5 (3.75mm) needles.
11-st chart rep measures approx 1¼"/3cm across.
Take time to check gauges.

Cable and Bobble Leg Warmers

BEGIN CHART

Set-up row (WS) P1, *[k1, p1, M1 p-st, p2] twice, [k1, p1] twice; rep from * 4 times more—71 sts.

Next row [K1, p1, k1, work row 1 of chart over 11 sts] 5 times, k1.

Next row P1, [work row 2 of chart over 11 sts, p1, k1, p1] 5 times.

Cont to work chart in this maner until row 8 is complete. Rep rows 1–8 twice more, then rep rows 1–4 once.

Next (inc) row (RS) [Kfb, kfb, k1, work row 5 of chart over 11 sts] 5 times, k1—81 sts.

Next row (WS) P1, *work row 6 of chart over 11 sts, [p1, k1] twice, p1; rep from * 4 times more.

Cont to work in this manner through chart row 8. Rep rows 1–8 twice more, then rep rows 1–4 once.

Next (inc) row (RS) *[Kfb] 4 times, k1, work row 5 of chart over 11 sts; rep from * 4 times more, k1—101 sts.

Next row (WS) P1, *work row 6 of chart over 11 sts, [p1, k1] 4 times, p1; rep from * 4 times more.

Cont to work in this manner until chart row 8 is complete. Rep rows 1–8 four times more, then rep rows 1–4 once.

Next (joining) row (RS) With circular needle, *[k1, p1] 5 times, [k1, p2tog, k1, p1] twice; rep from * 4 times more. Place marker for beg of rnd, sl last st from LH needle to beg of circular needle, k2tog to join—90 sts. Cont in k1, p1 rib as established for 2"/5cm. Bind off loosely in pat.

Finishing

Sew side seam from ankle to cuff. ■

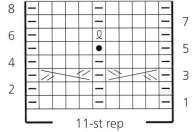

11-st rep

STITCH KEY

☐ k on RS, p on WS

─ p on RS, k on WS

 Q k1tbl

● make bobble (MB)

⧄ 4-st RC

⧅ 4-st LC

33

Tulip Lace Hat

A repeating motif of gentle curves evokes a cascade of tulips in a graceful, slightly slouchy hat.

DESIGNED BY JULIE GADDY

◖■■■▭

Knitted Measurements
**Brim circumference
(unstretched)**
18"/45.5cm
Length
8¾"/22cm

Materials
■ 1 3½oz/100g hank (each approx 307½yd/281m) of Cascade Yarns *Venezia Sport* (merino wool/mulberry silk) in #178 deep sea

■ One each sizes 5 and 6 (3.75 and 4mm) circular needle, 16"/40cm long, *or size to obtain gauge*

■ One set (4) size 6 (4mm) double-pointed needles (dpns)

■ Stitch marker

K1, P1 Rib
(over an even number of sts)
Rnd 1 *K1, p1; rep from * to end.
Rep rnd 1 for k1, p1 rib.

Lace Pattern
(multiple of 11 sts plus 10)
Rnd 1 *K2, yo, k1, yo, k5, p3tog; rep from * to last 10 sts, k2, yo, k1, yo, k5, remove marker, p3tog. Replace marker for new beg of rnd.
Rnd 2 and all even-numbered rnds Knit.
Rnd 3 *K1, yo, k3, yo, k4, p3tog; rep from * to last 10 sts, k1, yo, k3, yo, k4, remove marker, p3tog. Replace marker for new beg of rnd.
Rnd 5 *Yo, k5, yo, k3, p3tog; rep from * to last 10 sts, yo, k5, yo, k3, remove marker, p3tog. Replace marker for new beg of rnd.
Rnd 7 *K5, yo, k1, yo, k2, p3tog; rep from * to last 10 sts, k5, yo, k1, yo, k2, remove marker, p3tog. Replace marker for new beg of rnd.
Rnd 9 *K4, yo, k3, yo, k1, p3tog; rep from * to last 10 sts, k4, yo, k3, yo, k1, remove marker, p3tog. Replace marker for new beg of rnd.

Rnd 11 *K3, yo, k5, yo, p3tog; rep from * to last 10 sts, k3, yo, k5, yo, remove marker, p3tog. Replace marker for new beg of rnd.
Rnd 12 Knit.
Rep rnds 1–12 for lace pat.

Notes
1) As lace pat is worked, the marker will be removed at the end of each odd-numbered rnd and replaced after the last p3tog.
2) Change to dpns when there are too few sts to work comfortably on circular needle.

Hat
With smaller needle, cast on 120 sts. Place marker for beg of rnd and join, being careful not to twist sts.
Work in k1, p1 ribbing for 1"/2.5cm. Change to larger needle. Knit 1 rnd. Work rnds 1–12 of lace pat 3 times. Rep rnds 1–10 once more.

Gauge
22 sts and 32 rnds to 4"/10cm over lace pat after blocking using larger needles.
Take time to check gauge.

Tulip Lace Hat

Next (inc) rnd *K3, yo, k5, yo, p3tog; rep from * to last 10 sts, k3, yo, k5, yo, p2tog—121 sts. Knit 1 rnd. Hat measures approx 6 ½"/16.5cm from beg.

BEGIN CROWN SHAPING
Rnd 1 *K9, p2tog; rep from * to end—110 sts.
Rnds 2, 4, 6, 8, 10, and 12 Knit.
Rnd 3 *K8, p2tog; rep from * to end—99 sts.
Rnd 5 *K7, p2tog; rep from * to end—88 sts.
Rnd 7 *K6, p2tog; rep from * to end—77 sts.
Rnd 9 *K5, p2tog; rep from * to end—66 sts.
Rnd 11 *K4, p2tog; rep from * to end—55 sts.
Rnd 13 *K3, p2tog; rep from * to end—44 sts.
Rnd 14 *K2, p2tog; rep from * to end—33 sts.
Rnd 15 *K1, p2tog; rep from * to end—22 sts.
Rnd 16 P2tog around—11 sts.
Break yarn, leaving a long tail, and thread through rem sts. Pull tightly and secure end.

Finishing
Block hat to open lace, taking care not to stretch ribbed brim. ■

Quick Tip
To ensure that your hat is the correct length, block your lace swatch and be sure that you get the correct number of rows per inch.

34

Diamond Lattice Scarf

Garter stitch panels within a central lattice cable echo a garter stitch border for an elegant and unified design.

DESIGNED BY LEILA JACOB

Knitted Measurements
Width
5½"/14cm
Length excluding fringe
60"/152.5cm

Materials
■ 2 3½oz/100g hanks (each approx 219yd/200m) of Cascade Yarns *Venezia Worsted* (merino wool/mulberry silk) in #105 winterfresh

■ One pair size 7 (4.5mm) needles *or size to obtain gauge*

■ Cable needle (cn)

■ Size J/10 (6mm) crochet hook, to add fringe

Stitch Glossary
3-st RC Sl 1 st to cn and hold to *back*, k2, k1 from cn.
3-st LC Sl 1 st to cn and hold to *front*, k1, k1 from cn.
3-st RPC Sl 1 st to cn and hold to *back*, k2, p1, from cn.
3-st LPC Sl 2 sts to cn and hold to *front*, p1, k2 from cn.
4-st LC Sl 2 sts to cn and hold to *front*, k2, k2 from cn.

Scarf
Cast on 36 sts.
Next row (RS) K to last st, sl 1 knitwise. Rep this row 6 times more for garter st border pat.
Next (set-up) row (WS) K5, p8, [k1, p8] twice, k4, sl 1 knitwise.

BEG CHARTS
*Work row 1 of chart 1 over 36 sts. Cont to work chart in this manner until row 36 is complete.
Work row 1 of chart 2 over 36 sts. Cont to work chart in this manner until chart 2 is complete.
Rep from * 6 times more.
Work 7 rows in garter st border pat
Bind off.

Finishing
FRINGE (MAKE 26)
Cut 5 lengths of yarn, each 8"/20.5cm long. Holding 5 lengths tog, fold in half. With crochet hook, draw looped end through a stitch on 1 short end of scarf. Pull ends through loop and pull tight. Make 13 pieces of fringe for each end of scarf. ■

Gauge
26 sts and 35 rows to 4"/10cm over chart pat using size 7 (4.5mm) needles.
Take time to check gauge.

Diamond Lattice Scarf

CHART 1

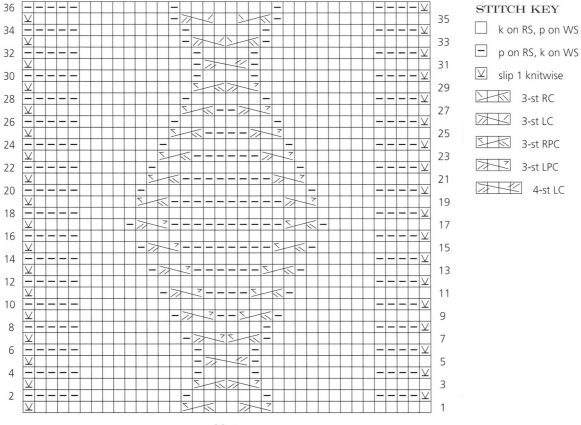

36 sts

STITCH KEY

☐	k on RS, p on WS
⊟	p on RS, k on WS
☑	slip 1 knitwise
	3-st RC
	3-st LC
	3-st RPC
	3-st LPC
	4-st LC

Quick Tip

Knitting charts are read from right to left when working RS rows, and from left to right when working WS rows.

102

34

Diamond Lattice Scarf

CHART 2

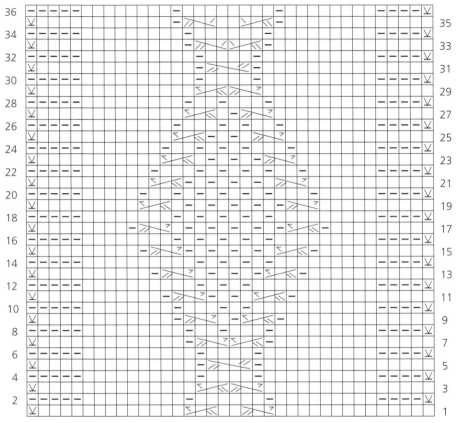

36 sts

STITCH KEY

☐ k on RS, p on WS

— p on RS, k on WS

☒ slip 1 knitwise

⟋⟍ 3-st RC

⟋⟍ 3-st LC

⟋⟍ 3-st RPC

⟋⟍ 3-st LPC

⟋⟍ 4-st LC

Reversible Fair Isle Cowl

Whether you're in the mood for simple stripes or fabulous Fair Isle, this cowl will have you covered.

DESIGNED BY MARY ANN STEPHENS

■■■□

Knitted Measurements
Circumference 22"/56cm
Height 7½"/19cm

Materials
- 1 3½oz/100g hank (each approx 307yd/281m) of Cascade Yarns *Venezia Sport* (merino wool/mulberry silk) each in #192 royal purple (MC) and #177 orchid haze (CC)
- One each sizes 4 and 5 (3.5 and 3.75mm) circular needle, 16"/40cm long, *or size to obtain gauge*
- Two size 2 (2.75mm) circular needles, 16"/40cm long, for garter st trim and joining
- Size E/4 (3.5mm) crochet hook
- Scrap yarn
- Stitch marker

Provisional Cast-on
With scrap yarn and crochet hook, chain the number of sts to cast on, plus a few extra. Cut a tail and pull the tail through the last chain. With knitting needle and yarn, pick up and knit the stated number of sts through the "purl bumps" on the back of the chain. To remove scrap chain, when instructed, pull out the tail from the last crochet st. Gently and slowly pull on the tail to unravel the crochet sts, carefully placing each released knit st on a needle.

Cowl
With size 2 (2.75mm) circular needle and MC, cast on 144 sts, using provisional cast-on method. Place marker for beg of rnd and join, being careful not to twist sts.
Work 6 rnds in garter st (k 1 rnd, p 1 rnd). Cont in garter st, work 2 rnds CC, 2 rnds MC.
Change to size 5 (3.75cm) needle.

BEGIN CHART
Rnd 1 Work 24-st rep 6 times around. Cont to work chart in this manner until rnd 28 is complete. Rep rnds 1–17 once more. Change to size 2 (2.75mm) needle. Work in garter st as foll: 2 rnds MC, 2 rnds CC, 6 rnds MC. Cut CC.

Gauges
26 sts and 35 rnds to 4"/10cm over St st using size 5 (3.75mm) needle.
26 sts and 32 rnds to 4"/10cm over chart pat using size 5 (3.75mm) needle.
Take time to check gauges.

Reversible Fair Isle Cowl

Lining Side

BEGIN LINING
Knit 1 rnd MC.
Change to size 4 (3.5mm) needle. Purl 1 rnd for turning ridge.
Work 42 rnds in St st. Change to CC and cont in St st until lining measures 1"/2.5cm shorter than motif side when folded along turning ridge. Change to MC and cont in St st until lining measures same as motif side when folded along turning ridge. Keep sts on needle.

Finishing
Carefully undo provisional cast-on and place sts on second size 2 (2.75mm) needle. Fold along turning ridge with WS tog. With lining side facing, join lining to cast-on edge as foll: With size 2 (2.75mm) needle and MC, [k 1 st from lining tog with 1 st from motif side] twice, *pass first st worked over 2nd st, k 1 st from lining tog with 1 st from motif side; rep from * until all sts have been bound off. ■

COLOR KEY

■ Royal purple (MC)

■ Orchid haze (CC)

28
27
25
23
21
19
17
15
13
11
9
7
5
3
1

24-st rep

Cable Cuff Mittens

Cables at the wrists converge into a single, striking central cable in a pair of warm and elegant mittens.

DESIGNED BY DEBBIE O'NEILL

■■■□

Size
Woman's Small/Medium

Knitted Measurements
Hand circumference
6 ½ (8 ¾)"/16.5 (22)cm
Length 10 ½ (11)"/26.5 (28)cm

Materials
■ 1 3½oz/100g hank (each approx 219yd/200m) of Cascade Yarns *Venezia Worsted* (merino wool/mulberry silk) in #126 lime
■ One set (4) size 4 (3.5mm) double-pointed needles (dpns) *or size to obtain gauge*
■ Cable needle (cn)
■ Scrap yarn
■ Stitch markers

Stitch Glossary
RT K the 2nd st on the LH needle without slipping to the RH needle, then k the first st. Sl both sts to RH needle.
LT K the 2nd st on the LH needle through the back loop, without slipping to the RH needle, then k the first st. Sl both sts to RH needle.

3-st RPC Sl 1 st to cn and hold to *back*, k2, p1 from cn.
3-st LPC Sl 2 sts to cn and hold to *front*, p1, k 2 from cn.
4-st RC Sl 2 sts to cn and hold to *back*, k2, k2 from cn.
4-st LC Sl 2 sts to cn and hold to *front*, k2, k2 from cn.
6-st RPC Sl 2 sts to cn and hold to *back*, k4, p2 from cn.
6-st LPC Sl 4 sts to cn and hold to *front*, p2, k4 from cn.

Left Mitten
Cast on 48 (64) sts and divide on 3 dpns. Place marker (pm) for beg of rnd and join, being careful not to twist sts.

BEGIN CHART 1
Rnd 1 Work 8-st rep 6 (8) times around. Cont to work chart in this manner until rnd 12 is complete. Rep rnds 1–12 once more, then rep rnds 1–8.

BEGIN CHART 2
Note Beg of rnd is at center of palm.
Next rnd K16 (24), work row 1 of chart 2 over next 16 sts, k to end of rnd. Cont to work chart in this way through rnd 6.

SHAPE GUSSET
Next (set-up) rnd K9 (15), pm, M1, k1, M1, k6 (8), work next chart row, k to end of rnd—2 sts inc'd.
Next rnd K to marker, sl marker, k to next marker, sl marker, k6 (8), work next chart rnd, k to end of rnd.
Next (inc) rnd K to marker, sl marker, M1, k to next marker, M1, sl marker, cont in pat to end of rnd—2 sts inc'd. Rep inc rnd every other rnd 5 (6) times more—15 (17) sts between gusset markers.
Work 2 rnds even.
Next rnd K to marker, place next 15 (17) sts on scrap yarn for thumb, cast on 3 sts, work to end of rnd—50 (66) sts in rnd.
Cont in pat through rnd 38, then rep rnds 1–38 until piece measures 8 ¾ (9 ¼)"/22 (23.5)cm from beg or 1 ¾"/4.5cm less than desired length of mitten.

SHAPE TOP
Next (set-up) rnd K13 (17), pm, k1, ssk, work 20 (28) sts in pat as established, k2tog, k1, pm, k to end of rnd—42 (64) sts.
Work 1 rnd even.

Gauge
27 sts and 36 rnds to 4"/10cm using size 4 (3.5mm) needles.
Take time to check gauge.

36

Cable Cuff Mittens

STITCH KEY

☐	k on RS, p on WS
⊟	p on RS, k on WS
⧖	RT
⧗	LT
	3-st RC
	3-st LC
	3-st RPC
	3-st LPC
	4-st RC
	4-st LC
	6-st RPC
	6-st LPC

CHART 1

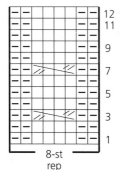

8-st rep

(rows numbered 1, 3, 5, 7, 9, 11, 12)

CHART 2

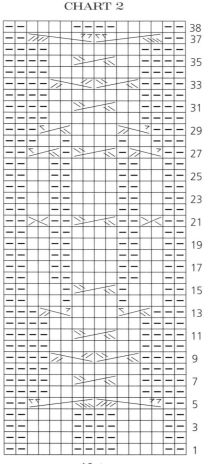

16 sts

(rows numbered 1–38)

Next (dec) rnd [K to 3 sts before marker, k2tog, k1, sl marker, k1, ssk] twice, k to end of rnd—4 sts dec'd.
Rep dec rnd every other rnd 5 (7) times more—24 (32 sts).
Divide sts on 2 dpns, keeping cable panel in center on front dpn. Graft closed using Kitchener st.

Thumb

Place 15 (17) thumb sts on dpns, pick up and k 5 sts along opening—20 (22) sts. Pm and work in St st until thumb measures 1¾"/4.5cm or ½"/1.5cm less than desired length of thumb.
Next (dec) rnd K to last 4 (3) sts, SK2P (k2tog), k1—18 (21) sts.
Work 1 rnd even.
Next (dec) rnd *K1, k2tog; rep from * around—12 (14) sts.
Work 1 rnd even.
Next (dec) rnd [K2tog] 6 (7) times—6 (7) sts.
Cut yarn and thread through rem 6 (7) sts.

Right Mitten

Work as for left mitten to shape gusset.

SHAPE GUSSET

Next (set-up) rnd K16 (24), work next chart rnd over 16 sts, k to last 10 (16) sts, pm, M1, K1, M1, pm, k to end of rnd—2 sts inc'd.
Work 1 rnd even.
Next (inc) rnd K16 (24), work next chart rnd over 16 sts, k to marker, sl marker, M1, k to next marker, M1, sl marker, k to end of rnd—2 sts inc'd.
Rep inc rnd every other rnd 5 (6) times more—15 (17) sts between gusset markers.
Work as for left mitten to shape top.

SHAPE TOP

Next (set-up) rnd K11 (15), pm, k1, ssk, work 20 (28) sts in pat as established, k2tog, k1, pm, k to end of rnd.
Complete as for left mitten. ■

Popcorn Cowl

A combination of bobbles and short rows forms a pretty
and whimsical alternating pleated pattern.

DESIGNED BY COURTNEY CEDARHOLM

Knitted measurements
Circumference
Approx 24"/61cm
Height
7"/18cm

Materials
■ 1 3½oz/100g hank (each approx
219yd/200m) of Cascade Yarns
Venezia Worsted (merino wool/mulberry
silk) in #159 ruby

■ One pair size 7 (4.5mm) needles *or
size to obtain gauge*

■ Spare size 7 (4.5mm) needle for
3-needle bind-off

■ Scrap yarn and crochet hook for
provisional cast-on

Stitch Glossary
MB (make bobble) ([K1, p1] twice) into
same st, turn, p4, turn, k4, turn and bind
off 4 sts purlwise, turn to cont row.

Short Row Wrap
and Turn (w&t)
on RS row (on WS row)
1) Wyib (wyif), sl next st purlwise.

2) Move yarn between the needles
to the front (back).
3) Sl the same st back to LH needle.
Turn work. One st is wrapped. Do *not*
hide (pick up) the wrap.

Provisional Cast-on
Using scrap yarn and crochet hook, chain
the number of sts to cast on, plus a few
extra. Cut a tail and pull the tail through
the last chain. With knitting needle and
yarn, pick up and knit the stated number

Gauge
20 sts and 34 rnds to 4"/10cm over St st using size 7 (4.5mm) needles.
Take time to check gauge.

Popcorn Cowl

of sts through the "purl bumps" on the back of the chain. To remove scrap chain, when instructed, pull out the tail from the last crochet st. Gently and slowly pull on the tail to unravel the crochet sts, carefully placing each released knit st on a needle.

3-Needle Bind-off

1) Hold right sides of pieces together on 2 needles. Insert 3rd needle knitwise into first st of each needle and wrap yarn knitwise.

2) Knit these 2 sts together and slip them off the needles. *Knit the next 2 sts together in the same manner.

3) Slip first st on 3rd needle over 2nd st and off needle. Rep from * in step 2 across row until all sts are bound off.

Short Row Sequence 1

Short row 1 (RS) K3, k2tog, yo, k19, w&t, p to end.

Short row 2 (RS) K2, k2tog, yo, k1, yo, SKP, k to wrapped st, w&t, p to end.

Short row 3 (RS) Rep short row 1.

Short row 4 K to wrapped st, w&t, p to end.

Row 5 (RS) K26, MB, k5, MB, k2.

Row 6 (WS) Purl. Rep rows 1–6 for short row sequence 1.

Short Row Sequence 2

Short row 1 (WS) P24, w&t, k19, yo, SKP, k to end.

Short row 2 (WS) P to the wrapped st, w&t, k17, k2tog, yo, k1, yo, SKP, k to end.

Short row 3 Rep short row 1.

Short row 4 P to the wrapped st, w&t, k to end.

Row 5 Purl.

Row 6 K2, MB, k5, MB, k to end. Rep rows 1–6 for short row sequence 2.

Cowl

Cast on 35 sts using provisional cast-on method. Knit 1 row. Purl 1 row.

BEGIN SHORT ROW SEQUENCES 1 & 2

*Work rows 1–6 of short row sequence 1 three times. Knit 1 row. Work rows 1–6 of short row sequence 2 three times. Purl 1 row. Rep from * 3 times more. Leave sts on needle and do not break yarn.

Finishing

Carefully unravel provisional cast-on and place open sts on a needle. With spare needle, join edges to form tube using 3-needle bind-off. ■

38

Stitch Sampler Scarf

Knit in a neutral palette and bordered by a garter stitch edge, simple blocks form a scarf that's greater than the sum of its parts.

DESIGNED BY CAROL SULCOSKI

■■☐☐

Knitted Measurements
Width
approx 6"/15cm
Length
approx 60½"/154.5cm

Materials
■ 1 3½oz/100g hank (each approx 219yd/200m) of Cascade Yarns *Venezia Worsted* (merino wool/mulberry silk) each in #132 mouse (A), #173 grey (B), and #110 pure diamond (C)

■ One pair size 7 (4.5mm) needles *or size to obtain gauge*

Scarf
BLOCK 1
With A, cast on 33 sts.
Next row (RS) Knit.
Next row K3, *p3, k3; rep from * to end. Rep last 2 rows until piece measures 8"/20.5cm from beg, end with a WS row. Break A.

BLOCK 2
Next row (RS) With B, knit.
Next row K3, p to last 3 sts, k3. Rep last 2 rows until block 2 measures 8"/20.5cm, end with a RS row. Break B.

BLOCK 3
Row 1 (WS) With C, k3, *p3, k3; rep from * to end.
Rows 2–4 K3, k the knit sts and p the purl sts to last 3 sts, k3.
Row 5 K3, *k3, p3, rep from * to last 3 sts, k3.
Rows 6–8 K3, k the knit sts and p the purl sts to last 3 sts, k3. Rep rows 1–8 until block 3 measures 8"/20.5cm, end with a WS row. Break C.

BLOCK 4
Next row (RS) With B, k3, p to the last 3 sts, k3.
Next row Knit. Rep last 2 rows until block 4 measures 8½"/21.5cm, end with a RS row. Break B.

BLOCK 5
Row 1 (WS) With A, k3, p to last 3 sts, k3.
Row 2 Knit.
Row 3 K6, *p3, k3; rep from * to last 3 sts, k3.

Row 4 *K3, p3; rep from * to last 3 sts, k3. Rep rows 1–4 until block 5 measures 9"/23cm, end with a row 1. Break A.

BLOCK 6
Row 1 (RS) With C, knit.
Row 2 K3, *p1, k1, p4; rep from * to last 6 sts, p1, k1, p1, k3.
Row 3 Knit.
Row 4 K3, *p4, k1, p1; rep from * to last 6 sts, p3, k3.
Rep rows 1–4 until block 6 measures 9"/23cm, end with a row 1 or 3.
Next row (WS) K3, p to last 3 sts, k3. Break C.

BLOCK 7
Next row With B, knit.
Row 1 (WS) K3, p to last 3 sts, k3.
Row 2 K3, *k2, sl 1 purlwise wyib; rep from * to last 3 sts, k3. Rep rows 1 and 2 until block 7 measures 10"/25.5cm, end with a row 1. Bind off. ■

Gauge
20 sts and 28 rows to 4"/10cm over St st using size 7 (4.5mm) needles.
Take time to check gauge.

Earflap Headband

Bright colorblocking adds to the sporty vibe
of this aviator-inspired ear warmer.

DESIGNED BY GALINA CARROLL

Knitted Measurements
Brim circumference
21"/53.5cm
Length of band
3½"/9cm
Length of earflap including band
9½"/24cm

Materials
■ 1 3½oz/100g hank (each approx 219yd/200m) of Cascade Yarns *Venezia Worsted* (merino wool/mulberry silk) each in #104 hot pepper (A), #117 bubble bath (B), and #196 lagoon (C)

■ Size 6 (4mm) circular needle, 16"/40cm long, *or size to obtain gauge*

■ Size E/4 (3.5mm) crochet hook

■ Stitch marker

Seed Stitch
(over an even number of sts)
Rnd 1 *P1, k1; rep from * to end.
Rnd 2 K the purl sts and p the knit sts.
Rep rnd 2 for seed st.

Twisted Cord
1) Cut 2 lengths of yarn 3 times the desired finished length and knot them about 1"/2.5cm from each end.
2) Insert a pencil or knitting needle through each end of the strands. Turn the strands clockwise until they are tightly twisted.
3) Keeping the strands taut, fold the piece in half. Remove the needles and allow the cords to twist onto themselves.

Headband
With A, cast on 90 sts. Place marker for beg of rnd and join, being careful not to twist sts. Work in seed st for 20 rnds.

EARFLAP
Next rnd With A, bind off 9 sts; break A, join B and work back and forth in pat over next 13 sts only for first earflap, keeping rem sts on hold. Cont in seed st over first earflap sts until 42 rows have been worked.

SHAPE EARFLAP
Next (dec) row (RS) K1, k2tog, work to last 3 sts, k2tog, k1—2 sts dec'd.
Dec 1 st each side every row for 4 rows more. Bind off rem 3 sts. Break B.
Rejoin A to cont rnd and bind off next 20 sts. Break A.
Join B and work second earflap same as first over next 13 sts.
Join A and bind off next 9 sts. Break A.

MOCK VISOR
With B, work in seed st over rem 26 sts until 21 rows have been worked.
Dec 1 st each side every row twice. Bind off rem 22 sts.

Finishing
Steam to block, if necessary.
With crochet hook and C, work 2 rnds of single crochet around entire edge of piece.
With C, make 2 twisted cords, each 11"/28cm long.
With C and B, make two 1"/2.5cm pompoms. Sew 1 pompom to each cord. Sew cord to each earflap.
Fold visor up, using photo as guide, and tack in place. ■

Gauge
17 sts and 23 rnds to 4"/10cm over seed st using size 6 (4mm) needles.
Take time to check gauge.

Twisted Cowl

A dramatically draped cowl with stripes and an open stitch pattern includes a twist—or two.

DESIGNED BY GEMMA WHYMS

Knitted Measurements
Circumference
approx 52"/132cm
Width
12"/30.5cm

Materials
■ 2 3½oz/100g hanks (each approx 219yd/200m) of Cascade Yarns *Venezia Worsted* (merino wool/mulberry silk) each in #123 dark bronze (A) and 132 mouse (B)

■ Size 7 (4.5mm) circular needle, 32"/80cm long, *or size to obtain gauge*

■ Stitch marker

Pattern Stitch
(multiple of 6 sts)
Rnd 1 Knit.
Rnd 2 *K3, pass first st knit over 2nd 2 sts, yo; rep from * around.
Rnd 3 Knit.
Rnd 4 K1, *yo, k3, pass first st knit over 2nd 2 sts; rep from * to last 2 sts, yo, k2, k1 from next rnd, pass first st knit over 2nd 2 sts, keep marker in place.
Rep rnds 1–4 for pat st.

Note
Break yarn for each color band. Do not carry color not being used up side of work.

Cowl
With A, cast on 240 sts. Carefully make 2 twists, place marker for beg of rnd, and join.
Work in pat st, changing colors as foll:
12 rnds A, 12 rnds B, 10 rnds A, 10 rnds B, 8 rnds A, 8 rnds B, 6 rnds A, 6 rnds B, 4 rnds A, 4 rnds B, 2 rnds A, 2 rnds B.
Bind off. ■

Gauge
18 sts and 28 rnds to 4"/10cm over pat st using size 7 (4.5mm) needles.
Take time to check gauge.

Criss-Cross Cable Scarf

A latticework of cables adds depth and dimension to a cozy scarf with lush fringe at the ends.

DESIGNED BY ALICIA KACHMAR

Knitted Measurements
Width
6"/15cm
Length excluding fringe
38"/96.5cm

Material
■ 2 3½oz/100g hanks (each approx 219yd/200m) of Cascade Yarns *Venezia Worsted* (merino wool/mulberry silk) in #117 bubble bath

■ One pair size 7 (4.5mm) needles *or size to obtain gauge*

■ Cable needle (cn)

■ Size J/10 (6mm) crochet hook, to add fringe

Stitch Glossary
4-st RC Sl 2 sts to cn and hold to *back*, k2, k2 from cn.
4-st LC Sl 2 sts to cn and hold to *front*, k2, k2 from cn.
4-st RPC Sl 2 sts to cn and hold to *back*, k2, p2 from cn.
4-st LPC Sl 2 sts to cn and hold to *front*, p2, k2 from cn.

Cable Pattern
(over 24 sts)
Row 1 (RS) K2, p8, 4-st RC, p8, k2.
Row 2 P2, k8, p4, k8, p2.
Row 3 [4-st LPC, p4, 4-st RPC] twice.
Row 4 [K2, p2, k4, p2, k2] twice.
Row 5 [P2, 4-st LPC, 4-st RPC, p2] twice.
Row 6 K4, p4, k8, p4, k4.
Row 7 P4, 4-st RC, p8, 4-st LC, p4.
Row 8 Rep row 6.
Row 9 [P2, 4-st RPC, 4-st LPC, p2], twice.
Row 10 Rep row 4.

Row 11 [4-st RPC, p4, 4-st LPC] twice.
Row 12 Rep row 2.
Rep rows 1–12 for cable pat.

Scarf
Cast on 48 sts.
Next row (RS) Work row 1 of cable pat twice across.
Cont to work pat in this manner until row 12 is complete.
Rep rows 1–12 until scarf measures approx 38"/96.5cm from beg.
Bind off.

Finishing
Cut 92 lengths of yarn, each 12"/30.5cm long. Holding 2 lengths tog, fold in half and draw looped end through a stitch on 1 short end of scarf. Pull ends through loop and pull tight. Make 23 pieces of fringe for each end of scarf. ■

Gauge
32 sts and 29 rows to 4"/10cm over cable pat using size 7 (4.5mm) needles.
Take time to check gauge.

Slouchy Seed Stitch Hat

A pale neutral allows rich textures to shine, including allover seed stitch and a ribbed brim set off with applied I-cord.

DESIGNED BY ANN MCCAULEY

Knitted Measurements
Brim circumference (unstretched)
18"/45.5cm
Length
9"/23cm

Materials
■ 1 3½oz/100g hank (each approx 219yd/200m) of Cascade Yarns *Venezia Worsted* (merino wool/mulberry silk) in #173 grey

■ One set (5) size 7 (4.5mm) double-pointed needles (dpns) *or size to obtain gauge*

■ Size 7 (4.5mm) circular needle, 16"/40cm long

■ Stitch marker

Stitch Glossary
Inc 1 Work into front and back of next st to maintain seed st pat while inc 1 st.

Seed Stitch
(over an even number of sts)
Rnd 1 *P1, k1; rep from * to end.
Rnd 2 K the purl sts and p the knit sts.
Rep rnd 2 for seed st.

K2, P2, Rib
(multiple of 4 sts)
Rnd 1 *P2, k2; rep from * around.
Rep rnd 1 for k2, p2 rib.

Note
Hat is begun with I-cord top knot and worked to the brim. The brim begins with applied I-cord; stitches are then picked up and worked in k2, p2 rib and finished with a 2nd round of applied I-cord.

Hat
I-CORD TOP KNOT
With 2 dpns, cast on 4 sts. Work rnd 1 of seed st. *Without turning work, slide the sts back to the opposite end of

Gauge
10 sts and 36 rnds to 4"/10cm over seed st using size 7 (4.5mm) needles.
Take time to check gauge.

Slouchy Seed Stitch Hat

marker, inc 1, sl marker] 8 times around—8 sts inc'd.
Work 1 rnd even in seed st.
Cont in seed st, rep inc rnd every other rnd 13 times more—128 sts.
Change to circular needle when necessary.
Place marker in last inc rnd.
Work even in seed st until piece measures 4"/10cm from marker, dec 8 sts evenly around in last rnd—120 sts.
Break yarn, leaving a long tail.

Brim
UPPER APPLIED I-CORD
With 2 dpns, cast on 4 sts.
Next row *K to last st on dpn, k last st tog tbl with 1 st from circular needle. *Without turning work, slide sts back to opposite end of needle to work next row from RS. Pull yarn tightly from end of row. Rep from * until all sts from circular needle have been worked into applied I-cord. Bind off 4 rem sts.

RIB
With circular needle, pick up and k 120 sts along the "ladders" formed by pulling the yarn across the back of the I-cord, pm for beg of rnd. Work 12 rnds in k2, p2 rib. Break yarn, leaving a long tail.

LOWER APPLIED I-CORD
With 2 dpns, cast on 5 sts, work as for upper applied I-cord.

Finishing
Curl I-cord stem at beg of hat, forming nub for top knot, and sew in place. ■

needle to work rnd 2 of seed st from RS. Pull yarn tightly from the end of the row. Rep from * until 13 rows of I-cord are complete.
Inc rnd 1 Inc 1 in each st around—8 sts.
Divide sts evenly on 4 dpns.
Work 1 rnd even in seed st.
Rep inc rnd 1—16 sts.
Next rnd [Work 2 sts, place marker (pm)] 8 times around.
Inc rnd 2 [Work in seed st to 1 st before

Cable and Rib Mitts

A wide cable-and-rib motif flows into ribbing at the tops and bottoms, in a cohesive and comfy mitt design.

DESIGNED BY DEBBIE O'NEILL

Size
Woman's Small/Medium

Knitted Measurements
Hand circumference
6½"/16.5cm
Length
6½"/16.5cm

Materials
- 1 3½oz/100g hank (each approx 307½yd/281m) of Cascade Yarns *Venezia Sport Multis* (merino wool/mulberry silk) in #205 teals
- One set (4) size 2 (2.75mm) double-pointed needles (dpns) *or size to obtain gauge*
- 2 cable needles (cn)
- Scrap yarn
- Stitch markers

Stitch Glossary
3-st RC Sl 1 st to cn and hold to *back*, sl next st to 2nd cn and hold to *back*, k1tbl, hold first cn in front of 2nd cn, p1 from 2nd cn, k1tbl from first cn.
3-st LC Sl 1 to cn and hold to *front*, sl next st to 2nd cn and hold to *back*, k1tbl, p1 from 2nd cn, k1tbl from first cn.

Left Mitt
Cast on 60 sts and divide evenly on 3 dpns. Place marker (pm) for beg of rnd and join, being careful not to twist sts.
Next rnd *K1tbl, p1; rep from * around for twisted rib.
Work 5 rnds more in twisted rib.

BEGIN CHART 1
Next rnd Work in rib for 19 sts, work rnd 1 of chart 1 over next 21 sts, work in rib to end.
Cont to work chart in this manner until rnd 8 is complete. Rep rnds 1–8 once more.

BEGIN CHART 2
Next rnd K19, work rnd 1 of chart 2 over 21 sts for cable panel, k to end.
Cont to work chart in this manner until rnd 8 of chart 2 is complete.
Read before cont to knit. Rep rnds 1–8 of chart 2 once more, then work rnds 1–8 of chart 1 over the 21 cable panel sts twice; AT THE SAME TIME, beg thumb gusset.

GUSSET
Set-up rnd K11, pm, M1, k1, M1, pm, work to end of rnd—62 sts.
Next rnd Work to 1st marker, sl marker, k to 2nd marker, sl marker, work to end of rnd.

Gauge
36 sts and 42 rnds to 4"/10cm over St st using size 2 (2.75mm) needles. *Take time to check gauge.*

Cable and Rib Mitts

CHART 1

21 sts

CHART 2

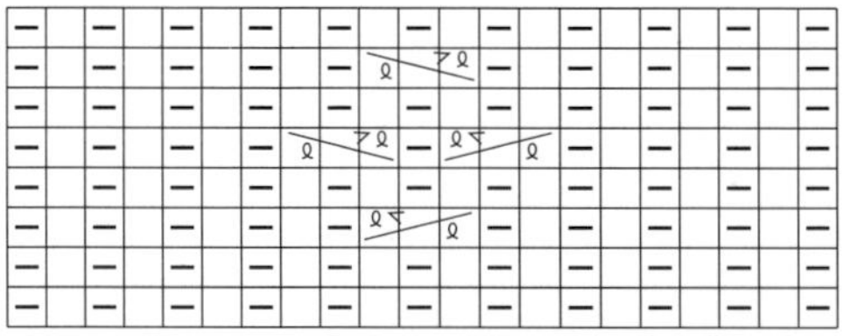

21 sts

STITCH KEY

☐ k1tbl

⊟ purl

3-st RC

3-st LC

Next (inc) rnd K to marker, sl marker, M1, k to marker, M1, sl marker, work to end of rnd—2 sts inc'd.
Rep inc rnd every other rnd 6 times more—17 sts between gusset markers.
Next rnd Work to 1st marker, place 17 sts on scrap yarn for thumb, cast on 2 sts, work to end of rnd—62 sts.
Next rnd K to chart sts, rep rnd 1 of chart 1, k to end of rnd.
Cont to work in this manner until rnd 8 of chart 1 is complete.
Next rnd K to cable panel sts, work in twisted rib as established over next 21 sts, k to end of rnd.
Cont in this manner until mitt measures 6"/15cm from beg. Work 4 rnds in twisted rib over all sts. Bind off in pat.

THUMB
Place 17 thumb sts on dpns, pick up and k 5 sts along cast-on sts of thumb opening, pm for beg of rnd—22 sts.
Divide sts evenly on dpns.
Knit 5 rnds.
Next (dec) rnd K18, S2KP, k1—20 sts.
Work until thumb measures ¼"/.5cm less than desired length of thumb. Work 2 rnds in twisted rib. Bind off in rib.

Right Mitt
Work as for left mitt to gusset.
Next rnd K to last 12 sts, pm for thumb gusset, M1, k1, M1, pm, work to end of rnd—2 sts inc'd.
Cont to end as for left mitt. ■

Striped Socks

An elegant stripe pattern and afterthought heel make these
socks a pleasure to knit and to wear.

DESIGNED BY YOKO HATTA

■■■□

Knitted Measurements
Foot circumference
7¾"/19.5cm
**Foot length from back of
heel to tip of toe**
9"/23cm
**Length from top of cuff
to bottom of heel**
10"/25.5cm

Materials
■ 1 3½oz/100g hank (each approx
307½yd/281m) of Cascade Yarns
Venezia Sport (merino wool/mulberry silk)
in #173 grey (A), #8400 charcoal (B),
and #193 power pink (C)

■ One set (4) each sizes 2 and 3
(2.75 and 3.25mm) double-pointed
needles (dpns) *or size to obtain gauge*

■ Scrap yarn

■ Stitch marker

K2, P2 Rib
(multiple of 4 sts)
Rnd 1 *K2, p2; rep from * around.
Rep rnd 1 for k2, p2 rib.

Stripe Pattern
In St st (k every rnd): 2 rnds B, 2 rnds C,
2 rnds A.
Rep these 6 rnds for stripe pat.

Socks
With A and larger needles, cast on
48 sts and divide on 3 dpns. Place marker
(pm) for beg of rnd and join, being careful
not to twist sts.
Work in k2, p2 rib until piece measures
2"/5cm from beg.
Knit 1 rnd with A.

BEGIN STRIPE PAT
Work in stripe pat until piece measures
approx 8"/20.5cm from beg, ending
with 2 rnds A.

AFTERTHOUGHT HEEL SET-UP
Next rnd With B, k24, with scrap yarn,
k24, slip scrap yarn sts back to LH needle
and knit them again with B.
Knit 1 rnd with B. Cont in stripe pat as
established until foot measures approx
5¼"/13.5cm from beg, end with 2 rnds B.

TOE
Change to smaller needles. Divide sts as
foll: 24 sts on dpn #1, 12 sts each
on dpn #2 and #3.

Next rnd With C, knit.
Next (dec) rnd Dpn #1: K1, k2tog, k to
last 3 sts, SKP, k1; dpn #2: k1, k2tog, k to
end of needle; dpn #3: k to last 3 sts,
SKP, k1—4 sts dec'd.
Rep dec rnd every other rnd 5 times
more—24 sts.
K the sts from dpn #3 to dpn #2. Break
yarn, leaving a long tail. Graft toe closed
using Kitchener st.

HEEL
Remove scrap yarn from heel and place
24 sts from upper edge of heel opening
on smaller dpn, place 24 sts from
lower edge of heel opening on a 2nd
smaller dpn.
With beg of rnd at LH side of lower edge
sts, divide sts on 3 dpns as foll: 24 sts on
dpn #1, 12 sts each on dpn #2 and #3.
Pm for beg of rnd.
Next rnd With B, knit.
Next (dec) rnd Dpn #1: K1, k2tog,
k to last 3 sts, SKP, k1; dpn #2:
k1, k2tog; dpn #3: k to last 3 sts, SKP,
k1—4 sts dec'd.
Rep dec rnd every other rnd 8 times
more—12 sts rem.
K the sts from dpn #3 to dpn #2.
Break yarn, leaving a long tail. Graft heel
closed using Kitchener st. ■

Gauge
25 sts and 36 rnds to 4"/10cm over St st using larger needles.
Take time to check gauge.

Mock Cable Scarf

A clever pattern of increases, decreases, and yarn overs produces
the look of a cable without the twist.

DESIGNED BY HOLLI YEOH

■■■▭

Knitted Measurements
Width
approx 7"/18cm
Length
approx 68"/172.5cm

Materials
■ 2 3½oz/100g hanks (each approx
219yd/200m) of Cascade Yarns
Venezia Worsted (merino wool/mulberry
silk) in #175 pink sapphire

■ One pair size 7 (4.5mm) needles
or size to obtain gauge

■ 4 stitch markers

Stitch Glossary
ssp Sl next 2 sts knitwise, one at a time
wyif, to RH needle. Insert tip of LH
needle into fronts of these sts and purl
them tog.

K1, P1 Rib
Row 1 (RS) Sl 1 wyib, *p1, k1; rep from *
to end of row.
Row 2 Sl 1 wyif, *k1, p1; rep from * to
end of row.
Rep rows 1 and 2 for K1, p1 rib.

Mock Cable Pattern
(over 51 sts)
Row 1 (RS) Sl 1 wyib, [p1, k1] 7 times,
k2tog, place marker (pm), [p1, k1] 3
times, p1, pm, k1, yo, p1, yo, k1, pm,
[p1, k1] 3 times, p1, pm, ssk, *k1, p1;
rep from * to last st, k1.
Row 2 Sl 1 wyif, work in rib to 2 sts
before marker, ssp, sl marker, work in rib
to next marker, sl marker, p1, yo, work in
rib to 1 st before next marker, being sure
to keep center st a k, yo, p1, sl marker,
work in rib to next marker, sl marker,
p2tog, work in rib to end.
Row 3 Sl 1 wyib, work in rib to 2 sts

before marker, k2tog, sl marker, work in
rib to next marker, sl marker, k1, yo,
work in rib to 1 st before next marker,
being sure to keep center st a p, yo, k1,
sl marker, work in rib to marker, sl
marker, ssk, work in rib to end.
Rows 4–15 Rep rows 2 and 3 six times
more.
Row 16 Ssp, remove marker, work in rib
to next marker, remove marker, p1, yo,
work in rib to 1 st before next marker, yo,
p1, remove marker, work in rib to next
marker, remove marker, p2tog.
Rep rows 1–16 for mock cable pat.

Scarf
Cast on 51 sts.
Work in k1, p1 rib, slipping first st of
every row, until scarf measures 2"/5cm
from beg, end with a WS row.

BEG MOCK CABLE PAT
Work row 1 of mock cable pat over 51
sts. Cont to work in this manner until
row 16 is complete.
Rep rows 1–16 of mock cable pat until
scarf measures approx 66"/167.5cm
from beg, end with a pat row 16.
Work in k1, p1 rib, slipping first st of
every row, for 2"/5cm.
Bind off. ■

Gauge
29 sts and 25 rows to 4"/10cm over mock cable pat using size 7 (4.5mm) needles.
Take time to check gauge.

Drop Stitch Mitts

A wavy rib created by dropped stitches softens the lines of a pair of long fingerless gloves.

DESIGNED BY RACHEL MAURER

■■■□

Knitted Measurements
Hand circumference (relaxed) 7"/18cm
Length 13¼"/33.5cm

Materials
■ 1 3½oz/100g hank (each approx 307½yd/281m) of Cascade Yarns *Venezia Sport* (merino wool/mulberry silk) in #196 lagoon
■ One set (5) size 3 (3.25mm) double-pointed needles (dpns) *or size to obtain gauge*
■ Scrap yarn
■ Stitch marker

Stitch Glossary
M1R Insert LH needle from back to front under strand between last st worked and next st on LH needle. K into front loop to twist st.
M1L Insert LH needle from front to back under strand between last st worked and next st on LH needle. K into back loop to twist st.
M1 p-st Insert needle from front to back under strand between last st worked and next st on LH needle. Purl into back loop to twist st.

K2, P3 Rib (multiple of 5 sts)
Rnd 1 *K2, p3; rep from * around.
Rep rnd 1 for k2, p3 rib.

K2, P2 Rib (multiple of 4 sts)
Rnd 1 *K2, p2; rep from * around.
Rep rnd 1 for k2, p2 rib.

Wavy Rib Pattern
(multiple of 8 sts)
Rnd 1 (RS) *K2, p1, M1 p-st, p1, k2, p2; rep from * around.
Rnds 2–6 *K2, p3, k2, p2; rep from * around.
Rnd 7 *K2, p1, drop next st, p1, k2, p2; rep from * around.
Rnd 8 *K2, p2, k2, p1, M1 p-st, p1; rep from * around.
Rnds 9–13 *K2, p2, k2, p3; rep from * around.
Rnd 14 *K2, p2, k2, p1, drop next st; rep from * around.
Rep rnds 1–14 for wavy rib pat.

MITTS (MAKE 2)
Cast on 60 sts and divide evenly on dpns. Place marker (pm) for beg of rnd and join, being careful not to twist sts.
Work 8 rnds in k2, p3 rib.
Next (dec) rnd *K2, p2tog, p1; rep from * around—48 sts.

Work in wavy rib pat until piece measures 8¼"/21cm from beg.

GUSSET
Next (set-up) rnd K1, pm, M1, pm, cont in pat to end of rnd—49 sts.
Next (inc) rnd K1, sl marker, M1R, k to marker, M1L, sl marker, work to end of rnd—2 sts inc'd.
Next 2 rnds K1, sl marker, k to marker, sl marker, work to end of rnd.
Rep inc rnd every 3rd rnd 7 times more—17 sts between markers, 65 sts in rnd.
Next rnd K1, place next 17 sts on scrap yarn, work to end of rnd.
Cont in wavy rib pat until piece measures approx 11½"/29cm from beg, end with a rnd 7 or 14.
Work 8 rnds in k2, p2 rib. Bind off in pat.

THUMB
Place sts from scrap yarn on dpns, pick up and k 2 sts along thumb opening, pm for beg of rnd, pick up and k 1 st along thumb opening—20 sts.
Next 2 (dec) rnds K2tog, k to last 2 sts, ssk—16 sts. Work 6 rnds in k2, p2 rib. Bind off in pat.

Finishing
Unravel all dropped sts. ■

Gauge
30 sts and 32 rows to 4"/10cm over wavy rib pat using size 3 (3.25mm) needles. *Take time to check gauge.*

Fair Isle Beret

Jewel tones evoke stained glass in a design that features Fair Isle panels and a corrugated rib brim.

DESIGNED BY HEIDI TODD KOZAR

Knitted Measurements
Brim circumference (unstretched)
18"/45.5cm
Diameter at widest point
10"/25.5cm

Materials
■ 1 3½oz/100g hank (each approx 307½yd/281m) of Cascade Yarns *Venezia Sport* (merino wool/mulberry silk) each in #179 peacock blue (A), #159 ruby (B), and #196 lagoon (C)

■ One each sizes 4 and 5 (3.5 and 3.75mm) circular needle, 16"/40cm long, *or size to obtain gauge*

■ One set (4) size 5 (3.75mm) double-pointed needles (dpns)

■ Stitch marker

Corrugated Rib
(multiple of 4 sts)
Rnd 1 *K2 B, p2 A; rep from * around. Rep rnd 1 for corrugated rib.

Beret
With smaller needle and C, cast on 112 sts. Place marker for beg of rnd and join, being careful not to twist sts.
Next rnd With C, *k2, p2; rep from * around.
Join B and work 9 rnds in corrugated rib. Change to larger needle.
Next (inc) rnd With C, knit, inc 48 sts evenly around—160 sts.

BEGIN CHART 1
Next rnd Work 8-st chart rep 20 times around.
Cont to work in this manner until rnd 13 of chart 1 is complete.

BEGIN CHART 2
Note Change to dpns when there are too few sts to fit comfortably on circular needle.

Next rnd Work chart rep 8 times around. Cont to foll chart in this manner until rnd 35 is complete. Note that the final S2KP in the dec rnds is worked with the last st of the rnd and the first 2 sts of the next rnd—16 sts.
Rnd 36 With C, [k2tog] 8 times around. Break yarn, leaving a long tail, and thread through rem 8 sts to close.

Finishing
To block, with C, sew a running st above cast-on rnd all the way around. Wet hat and place on a 12"/30.5cm dinner plate. Draw running thread until corrugated ribbing is drawn up but still lying flat. Let dry. Remove running thread from ribbing, then remove beret from plate. ■

Gauge
22 sts and 30 rnds to 4"/10cm over Fair Isle pat using larger needles.
Take time to check gauge.

Fair Isle Beret

CHART 2

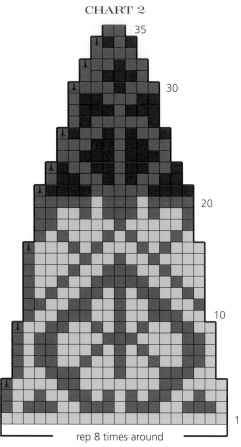

35

30

20

10

1

rep 8 times around

CHART 1

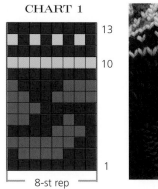

13

10

1

8-st rep

COLOR & STITCH KEY

 Peacock blue (A)

Ruby (B)

Lagoon (C)

S2KP

Knotted I-Cord Belt

I-cord worked around cotton cording and twisted into a knot transforms a wide elastic band into a beautiful statement belt.

DESIGNED BY ALEX CAPSHAW-TAYLOR

Knitted Measurements
I-cord braid with sl st bands
approx 4 x 8½"/10 x 21.5cm

Materials
- 1 3½oz/100g hank (each approx 219yd/200m) of Cascade Yarns *Venezia Worsted* (merino wool/mulberry silk) in #124 bear
- 2 size 5 (3.75mm) double-pointed needles (dpns) *or size to obtain gauge*
- 3"/7.5cm-wide elastic for desired waist measurement, allowing 1"/2.5cm overlap at center of back, in color to match yarn
- 2⅝ yd/2.5m of 5.5mm cotton cording
- 3 buttons, ¾"/19mm diameter
- 3 snaps, ½"/12mm diameter
- Sewing needle and thread to match yarn

Notes
1) Pieces are worked separately and sewn in place.
2) Stitches are slipped purlwise.

Slip Stitch Pattern
(multiple of 2 sts plus 1)
Row 1 (RS) K1, *sl 1 wyif, k1; rep from * to end.
Row 2 P2, *sl 1 wyib, p1; rep from * to end.
Rep rows 1 and 2 for sl st pat.

Belt
Cut 6 pieces of cotton cording, 2 each 15"/38cm (A and D), 16"/40.5cm (B and E), and 16¼"/41cm (C and F). With dpns and yarn, cast on 3 sts.
*Knit 1 row. Without turning work, slide sts back to opposite end of needle to work next row from RS. Pull yarn tightly from end of row. Rep from * until 3 rows of I-cord have been worked.
Next (inc) row [K1, M1] twice, k1—5 sts. Slip 1 length of cotton cording into beg of I-cord. Cont to work I-cord around cotton cording until cording is completely covered.
Next (dec) row K2tog, k1, k2tog—3 sts. Knit 3 rows of I-cord. Bind off.
Rep for rem pieces of cotton cording.

FRONT BANDS (MAKE 2)
Cast on 7 sts. Do not join. Work in sl st pat until piece measures 6½"/16.5cm from beg. Bind off.

BACK BANDS (MAKE 2)
Cast on 23 sts. Do not join. Work in sl st pat until piece measures 4"/10cm from beg. Bind off.

Gauge
28 sts and 44 rows to 4"/10cm over sl st pat using size 5 (3.75mm) needles.
Take time to check gauge.

Knotted I-Cord Belt

48

Finishing

Block front bands to
1 x 6½"/2.5 x 16.5cm.
Block back bands to
3¼ x 4"/8.5 x 10cm.

Fold back band in half with WS tog and place one end of elastic in the fold. With sewing needle and thread, sew in place through all layers and around all edges. Rep for other end. Sew 3 buttons on RS of right back band, placing top button ¼"/.5cm from upper edge, bottom button ¼"/.5cm from lower edge, and center button evenly spaced between.
Sew 3 female snaps on WS of right back band to correspond to buttons. Sew male snaps on RS of left back band opposite female snaps. Arrange I-cord pieces into center knot, using labeled photo as guide. Line up flat ends of I-cords with center of front bands and sew in place.
To keep I-cords from slipping, use sewing needle and thread to tack together. Sew front bands to front of elastic so that knot is at center. ∎

Button Cable Beret

Monochromatic buttons are worked cleverly into a cable pattern for a quick and quirky embellishment.

DESIGNED BY KIM HAESEMEYER

Knitted Measurements
Brim circumference
20"/51cm
Diameter at widest point
11"/28cm

Materials
■ 1 3½oz/100g hank (each approx 307½yd/281m) of Cascade Yarns *Venezia Sport* (merino wool/mulberry silk) in #101 white heaven

■ One each sizes 5 and 7 (3.75 and 4.5mm) circular needle, 16"/40cm long, *or size to obtain gauge*

■ One set (4) size 7 (4.5mm) double-pointed needles (dpns)

■ Cable needle (cn)

■ 60 buttons, ¾"/19mm diameter

■ 10 buttons, ½"/12mm diameter

■ Sewing needle and thread to match buttons

■ Stitch markers

Stitch Glossary
10-st RC Sl 5 sts to cn and hold to *back*, k5, k5 from cn.
10-st LC Sl 5 sts to cn and hold to *front*, k5, k5 from cn.

K2, P2 Rib
(multiple of 4 sts)
Rnd 1 *K2, p2; rep from * around.
Rep rnd 1 for k2, p2 rib.

Double Cable Pattern
(multiple of 24 sts)
Rnd 1 *P2, 10-st RC, 10-st LC, p2; rep from * around.
Rnds 2–12 *P2, k20, p2; rep from * around.
Rep rnds 1–12 for double cable pat.

Beret
With smaller needle, cast on 120 sts. Place marker (pm) and join, being careful not to twist sts. Work in k2, p2 rib for 1¼"/3cm. Change to larger needle.
Next (inc) rnd *Kfb; rep from * around—240 sts.

Gauges
23 sts and 30 rows to 4"/10cm over St st using size 7 (4.5mm) needles.
One 24-st rep of double cable pat worked in rnds measures 3"/7.5cm.
Take time to check gauges.

140

Button Cable Beret

BEGIN DOUBLE CABLE PAT
Next rnd Work rnd 1 of double cable pat, working the 24-st rep 10 times around.
Cont to work pat in this way through rnd 12. Rep rnds 1–12 twice more, then rep rnd 1 once more.

SHAPE CROWN
Note Change to dpns when there are too few sts to fit comfortably on needle.
Set-up rnd [P2, k20, pm, p2] 9 times, p2, k20, p2.
Next (dec) rnd [P2, S2KP, work to 3 sts before marker, S2KP, p2, sl marker] 10 times—40 sts dec'd.
Rep dec rnd every other rnd 3 times more—80 sts.
Work one rnd even.
Next (dec) rnd [P2, sl 2, k2tog, pass 2 sl sts over the k2tog to dec 3 sts, p2] 10 times—50 sts.
Next rnd [P2, k1, p2] 10 times.
Next (dec) rnd [P2tog tbl, k1, p2tog] 10 times—30 sts.
Next rnd [P1, k1, p1] 9 times, p1, k1, pm for new beg of rnd.
Next rnd [P2tog tbl, k1] 10 times—20 sts.
Next rnd [P1, k1] 10 times.
Next (dec) rnd [K2tog] 10 times—10 sts.
Break yarn, leaving a long tail.
Thread tail through open sts twice and pull tight to close.

Finishing
Wet block, taking care not to stretch ribbed brim.
Using photo as guide, sew 3 larger buttons to the center of each double cable rep. Sew 3 larger buttons in each column of purl sts between cables at the cable cross row. Sew 1 smaller button to the center of each double cable at the top of the hat. ■

50

Diamonds Shawl

Elegant diamond-shaped lace motifs and an intricate edging form a shawl that will turn heads.

DESIGNED BY MANDA SHAH

Knitted Measurements
Width along upper edge after blocking
56"/142cm
Height at center including edging after blocking
29"/73.5cm

Materials
■ 2 3½oz/100g hanks (each approx 307½yd/281m) of Cascade Yarns *Venezia Sport* (merino wool/mulberry silk) in #8400 charcoal

■ Size 5 (3.75mm) circular needle, 24"/61cm long, *or size to obtain gauge*

Stitch Glossary
Wrap 3 sts Wyib, sl 3 sts, move yarn to front, sl the 3 sts back to LH needle, move yarn to back and k3.
Make 3 from 1 K1tbl and leave on LH needle, k same st in front loop and drop both sts from needle, insert LH needle from front to back in front loop of st below the 2 sts just knit and k1tbl—2 sts inc'd.

Edging Pattern
(begin with 8 sts)
Row 1 (RS) Sl 1, k2, yo, k2tog, [yo] twice, k2tog, k1—9 sts.
Row 2 K3, p1, k2, yo, k2tog, k1.
Row 3 Sl 1, k2, yo, k2tog, k1, [yo] twice, k2tog, k1—10 sts.
Row 4 K3, p1, k3, yo, k2tog, k1.
Row 5 Sl 1, k2, yo, k2tog, k2, [yo] twice, k2tog, k1—11 sts.
Row 6 K3, p1, k4, yo, k2tog, k1.
Row 7 Sl 1, k2, yo, k2tog, k to end.
Row 8 Bind off 3 sts, k to last 3 sts, yo, k2tog, k1—8 sts.
Rep rows 1–8 for edging pat.

Notes
1) Shawl is worked from the lower point to the upper edge.
2) Piece is worked back and forth in rows. Circular needle is used to accommodate large number of sts. Do not join.

Gauge
17 sts and 30 rows to 4"/10cm over St st after blocking using size 5 (3.75mm) needles.
Take time to check gauge.

Diamonds Shawl

STITCH KEY

☐	k on RS, p on WS
♈	make 3 from 1
⟋	k2tog
⟍	SKP
O	yo
℧	k1tbl
⊼	S2KP
⟋	SK2P
⟍	p3tog
⟋ ⟍	k3tog
⟍	k3tog tbl
⊏━━▶	wrap 3 sts

3) Edging is worked separately and sewn to side edges of shawl when complete.

Shawl
Cast on 9 sts.

BEGIN CHART 1
Work rows 1–18 of chart 1—29 sts.

BEGIN CHART 2
Work chart 2 until row 36 is complete—69 sts.
Rep rows 1–36 of chart 2 as foll:
Work to rep line, work 20-st rep 3 times across, work to end of chart—109 sts.
When row 36 of chart 2 is complete, rep rows 1–36 twice more in this manner, working 2 additional 20-st reps each time the 36-row rep is complete—189 sts.
Knit 2 rows. Bind off loosely.

Finishing
EDGING
Cast on 8 sts. Knit 1 WS row.
Work in edging pat until edging fits along edge of shawl from one side of upper edge around lower point, to opposite side of upper edge. Sew edging to sides of shawl.
Block shawl to measurements, pinning points of edging separately. ■

CHART 1

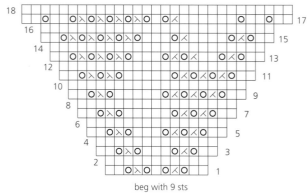

beg with 9 sts

50

Diamonds Shawl

CHART 2

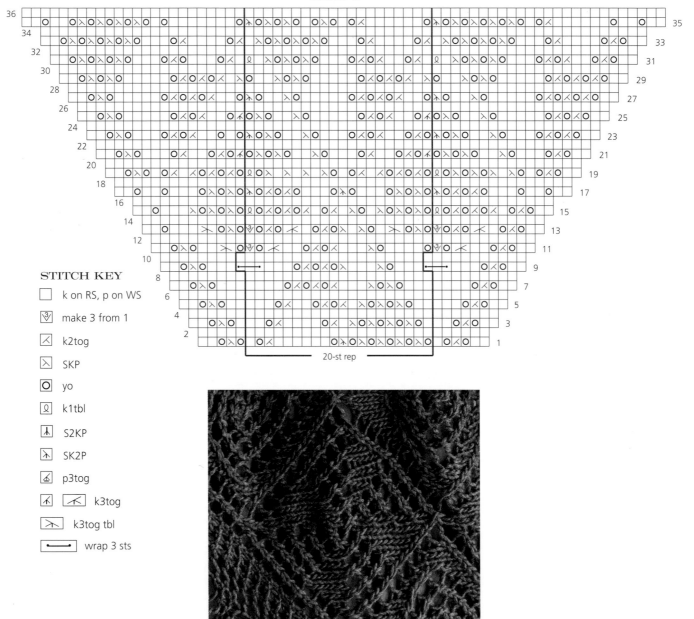

STITCH KEY

☐	k on RS, p on WS
⩔	make 3 from 1
╱	k2tog
╲	SKP
⊙	yo
Ω	k1tbl
⟂	S2KP
⟙	SK2P
◢	p3tog
⟀ ⟍	k3tog
⟋	k3tog tbl
▬	wrap 3 sts

20-st rep

Crossing Cables Hat

A pattern of overlapping cables from brim to crown feels at once luxe and cozy.

DESIGNED BY FAINA GOBERSTEIN

◼◼◼▢

Knitted Measurements
Brim circumference (unstretched)
18"/45.5cm
Height 8"/20.5cm

Materials
- 1 3½oz/100g hank (each approx 307½yd/281m) of Cascade Yarns *Venezia Sport Multis* (merino wool/mulberry silk) in #208 citrus cream
- One set (5) each sizes 3 and 5 (2.75 and 3.75mm) double-pointed needles (dpns) *or size to obtain gauge*
- Cable needle (cn)
- Stitch marker

Stitch Glossary
2-st RC Sl 1 st to cn and hold to *back*, k1, k1 from cn.
2-st LC Sl 1 st to cn and hold to *front*, k1, k1 from cn.
4-st RC Sl 2 sts to cn and hold to *back*, k2, k2 from cn.
4-st LC Sl 2 sts to cn and hold to *front*, k2, k2 from cn.
5-st RC Sl 2 sts to cn and hold to *back*, k3, k2 from cn.
7-st RC Sl 3 sts to cn and hold to *back*, k4, k3 from cn.

Twisted Rib
(over an even number of sts)
Rnd 1 *K1tbl, p1; rep from * to end.
Rep rnd 1 for twisted rib.

Hat
With smaller needles, cast on 142 sts. Place marker (pm) for beg of rnd and join, being careful not to twist sts. Work 10 rnds in twisted rib.
Next (inc) rnd Knit, inc 10 sts evenly spaced around—152 sts.
Change to larger needles.

BEGIN CHART 1
Rnd 1 Work 19-st rep of chart 1 for 8 times around.
Cont to work chart in this manner until rnd 22 is complete. Rep rnds 3–18 once more. Hat measures approx 4½"/11cm from beg.

BEGIN CHART 2
Work rnd 1 of chart 2 for 8 times around. Cont to work chart in this manner until rnd 18 is complete—88 sts.

CROWN SHAPING
Next (dec) rnd [2-st RC, p1, sl 2 sts to cn and hold to *back*, k2tog, k1, k2 from cn, p1, 2-st LC] 8 times around—80 sts.

Gauge
34 sts and 40 rnds to 4"/10cm over chart 1 pat using larger needles.
Take time to check gauge.

Crossing Cables Hat

CHART 1

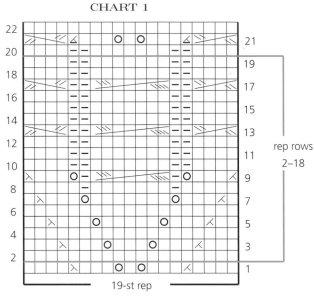

19-st rep

rep rows 2–18

CHART 2

rep 8 times around

STITCH KEY

☐	k on RS, p on WS
⊟	p on RS, k on WS
⟋	k2tog
⟍	SKP
◺	p2tog
O	yo
⧓	2-st RC
⧓	2-st LC
⧓	4-st RC
⧓	4-st LC
⧓	5-st RPC
⧓	7-st RC

Next rnd [K2, p1, k4, p1, k2] 8 times around.

Next (dec) rnd [K1, p2tog, k4, p2tog, k1] 8 times around—64 sts.

Next (dec) rnd [K1, p1, sl 2 sts to cn and hold to *back*, k2, k2tog, p1, k1 from cn] 8 times around—56 sts.

Next rnd [K1, p1, k3, p1, k1] 8 times around.

Next (dec) rnd [K1, p1, k2tog, k1, p1, k1] 8 times around—48 sts.

Next rnd [K1, p1, k2, p1, k1] 8 times around.

Next (dec) rnd [K1, p1, k2tog, p1, k1] 7 times, k1, p1, k2tog, pm for new beg of rnd—40 sts.

Next (dec) rnd [K2tog, p1, k1, p1] 8 times around—32 sts.

Next rnd *K1, p1; rep from * to end.

Next (dec) rnd [K2tog] 8 times around—16 sts.

Break yarn, leaving a long tail. Thread through rem sts. Pull tightly to close. ∎

52
Bow Clutch

This charming clutch can complement any style, from sophisticated vintage to sweet and feminine.

DESIGNED BY DEVIN COLE

■■■□

Knitted Measurements
Width
approx 12"/30.5cm
Height
approx 6½"/16.5cm

Materials
■ 1 3½oz/100g hank (each approx 219yd/200m) of Cascade Yarns *Venezia Worsted* (merino wool/mulberry silk) in #104 hot pepper (MC)

■ 1 3½oz/100g hank (each approx 307½yd/281m) of Cascade Yarns *Venezia Sport* (merino wool/mulberry silk) in #132 mouse (CC)

■ One pair each sizes 4, 7, 8, and 9 (3.5, 4.5, 5, and 5.5mm) needles *or size to obtain gauge*

■ One 12"/30.5cm non-separating zipper

■ Sewing needle and thread

■ Stitch markers

Stitch Glossary
LIR (lifted inc right) K1 without dropping st from LH needle, insert tip of RH needle in st below st just knit and k1, drop both sts from LH needle.
LIL (lifted inc left) Insert RH needle from the top down into st below next st on LH needle, k this st, then k the st on LH needle.

Seed Stitch
(over an even number of sts)
Row 1 (RS) *K1, p1; rep from * to end.
Row 2 P the knit sts and k the purl sts.
Rep row 2 for seed st.

Clutch
BACK
With size 7 (4.5mm) needles and MC, cast on 54 sts. Beg with a RS row, work 2 rows in St st.
Next (inc) row (RS) [LIR] twice, k to last 2 sts, [LIL] twice—4 sts inc'd.
Rep inc row every other row once more. Purl one row.
Next (inc) row (RS) LIR, k to last st, LIL—64 sts.
Change to size 8 (5mm) needles.
Next row [P16, place marker (pm)] 3 times, p16.

Gauge
20 sts and 28 rows to 4"/10cm over St st using size 7 (4.5mm) needles.
Take time to check gauge.

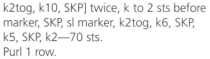

k2tog, k10, SKP] twice, k to 2 sts before marker, SKP, sl marker, k2tog, k6, SKP, k5, SKP, k2—70 sts.
Purl 1 row.

Next (dec) row (RS) [K to 2 sts before marker, SKP, sl marker, k2tog] 3 times, k to end—6 sts dec'd.
Rep last 2 rows once more—58 sts.
Work even for 2"/5cm more. Bind off.

FRONT
Work same as back.

UPPER BAND
With size 4 (3.5mm) needles and CC, cast on 172 sts. Work in seed st until band measures 2"/5cm from beg.
Bind off.

BOW
With size 4 (3.5mm) needles and CC, cast on 50 sts. Work in seed st until piece measures 3½"/9cm from beg. Bind off. Tie piece in a knot in the center to form bow.

Finishing
Sew side and bottom seams of bag, leaving upper (bound-off) edge open. With CC, sew short ends of band together. Sew bow to band, covering seam. Placing band so that bow is at center front of bag and using photo as guide, sew band to upper edge of bag along both edges of band.
With sewing needle and thread, sew zipper along top edges of bag. ■

Next (inc) row (RS) [K to 1 st before marker, LIR, sl marker, LIL] 3 times, k to end—6 sts inc'd.
Rep inc row every other row 4 times more—94 sts.
Work 3 rows even.
Rep inc row once more—100 sts.
Work 4 rows even.
Change to size 9 (5.5mm) needles.
Purl 1 row.
Next (dec) row (RS) K2, SKP, k7, SKP, [k to 2 sts before marker, SKP, sl marker, k2tog, k11, SKP] twice, k to 2 sts before marker, SKP, sl marker, k2tog, [k7, k2tog] twice, k2—86 sts.
Purl 1 row.
Change to size 7 (4.5mm) needles.
Next (dec) row (RS) K2, SKP, k5, SKP, [k to 2 sts before marker, SKP, sl marker,

Quick Tip
This clutch knits up quickly. Make a few in different colors for an evening bag to go with any ensemble.

53

Diamond Motif Shawlette

Diamonds built on one another by picking up stitches are
prettified by an edging of ruffles and eyelets.

DESIGNED BY DIANE ZANGL

Knitted Measurements
32 x 18"/81 x 45.5cm including border

Materials
■ 2 3½oz/100g hanks (each approx
307½yd/281m) of Cascade Yarns
Venezia Sport Multis (merino
wool/mulberry silk) in #206 autumn

■ One pair size 7 (4.5mm) needles
or size to obtain gauge

■ Size 7 (4.5mm) circular needle,
42"/107cm long

■ Stitch marker

Note
Use diagram as guide for diamond
number and placement.

Shawl
DIAMOND 1
Cast on 35 sts. Place marker in center st
and move this marker up every row.
Row 1 and all WS rows Purl.
Row 2 K2, [yo, k2tog] 7 times, S2KP,
[ssk, yo] 7 times, k2—33 sts.
Row 4 P to 1 st before marked st, S2KP,
p to end—31 sts.
Row 6 K2, [yo, k2tog] 6 times, S2KP,
[ssk, yo] 6 times, k2—29 sts.
Row 8 Rep row 4—27 sts.

Row 10 K2, [yo, k2tog] 5 times, S2KP,
[ssk, yo] 5 times, k2—25 sts.
Row 12 Rep row 4—23 sts.
Row 14 K2, [yo, k2tog] 4 times, S2KP,
[ssk, yo] 4 times, k2—21 sts.
Row 16 Rep row 4—19 sts.
Row 18 K2, [yo, k2tog] 3 times, S2KP,
[ssk, yo] 3 times, k2—17 sts.
Row 20 Rep row 4—15 sts.
Row 22 K2, [yo, k2tog] twice, S2KP,
[ssk, yo] twice, k2—13 sts.
Row 24 Rep row 4—11 sts.
Row 26 K2, yo, k2tog, S2KP, ssk, yo,
k2—9 sts.
Row 28 Rep row 4—7 sts.
Row 30 K2, S2KP, k2—5 sts.
Row 32 K1, S2KP, k1—3 sts.
Row 34 S2KP. Break yarn and fasten
off last st.

DIAMOND 2 (4, 7, 11, AND 16)
Cast on 18 sts. With RS facing, pick up
and k 17 sts along top RH edge of
diamond 1 (2, 4, 7, 11)—35 sts.
Place marker in center st and move this
marker up every row. Complete as for
diamond 1.

Gauge
16 sts and 32 rows to 4"/10cm over diamond pat using size 7 (4.5mm) needles.
Take time to check gauge.

Diamond Motif Shawlette

DIAMOND 3 (6, 10, 15, AND 19)
With RS facing, pick up and k 17 sts along top LH edge of diamond 1 (3, 6, 10, 15), cast on 18 sts—35 sts. Place marker in center st and move this marker up every row. Complete as for diamond 1.

DIAMOND 5 (8, 9, 12, 13, 14, 17, 18, 20, AND 21)
With RS facing, pick up and k 17 sts along top LH edge of diamond 2 (4, 5, 7, 8, 9, 11, 14, 16, 18), 1 st in point of diamond 1 (2, 3, 4, 5, 6, 7, 10, 11, 15), 17 sts along top RH edge of diamond 3 (5, 6, 8, 9, 10, 12, 15, 17, 19)—35 sts. Place marker in center st and move this marker up every row. Complete as for diamond 1.

HALF DIAMOND 22 (23)
With RS facing, pick up and k 17 sts along top RH edge of diamond 12 (13), 1 st in point of diamond 8 (9), 17 sts along top RH edge of diamond 13 (14)—35 sts.
Row 1 and all WS rows P2tog, p to last 2 sts, p2tog tbl.
Row 2 Ssk, k1, [yo, k2tog] 6 times, S2KP, [ssk, yo] 6 times, k1, k2tog—29 sts.
Row 4 P2tog, p to 1 st before marked st, S2KP, p to last 2 sts, p2tog tbl—23 sts.
Row 6 Ssk, k1, [yo, k2tog] 3 times, S2KP, [ssk, yo] 3 times, k1, k2tog—17 sts.
Row 8 Rep row 4—11 sts.
Row 10 Ssk, k1, S2KP, k1, k2tog—5 sts.
Row 12 S2KP.
Break yarn and fasten off last st.

RUFFLED EYELET BORDER
With circular needle and RS facing, beg at center back neck, pick up and k 1 st in each st, and 1 st in every other row around entire shawl. Place marker for beg of rnd.
Rnd 1 Purl.
Rnd 2 *Yo twice, k1; rep from * around.
Rnd 3 Purl around, working first yo and dropping 2nd yo. Bind off knitwise. ∎

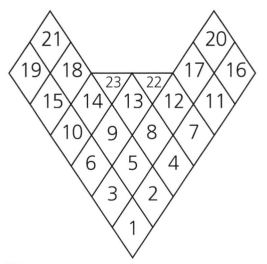

Ruffled Collar

Add a dash of whimsy to a warm collar with bright colors and an oversize Victorian-inspired ruffle.

DESIGNED BY ROBYN M. SCHRAGER

Knitted Measurements
Neck circumference
16 ½"/42cm
Length excluding ruffle
approx 7"/18cm

Materials
■ 1 3½oz/100g hank (each approx 307½yd/281m) of Cascade Yarns *Venezia Sport* (merino wool/mulberry silk) each in #179 peacock blue (A) and #193 power pink (B)

■ Size 4 (3.5mm) circular needle, 16"/40.5cm long, *or size to obtain gauge*

■ Size E/4 (3.5mm) crochet hook

■ Scrap yarn

■ Cable needle (cn)

Stitch Glossary
Kw2 K1, wrapping yarn twice around needle.

Provisional Cast-on
Using scrap yarn and crochet hook, chain the number of sts to cast on, plus a few extra. Cut a tail and pull the tail through the last chain. With knitting needle and yarn, pick up and knit the stated number of sts through the "purl bumps" on the back of the chain. To remove scrap chain, when instructed, pull out the tail from the last crochet st. Gently and slowly pull on the tail to unravel the crochet sts, carefully placing each released knit st on a needle.

Slip Stitch Pattern
(multiple of 8 sts)
Rnd 1 With A, *kw2, k4, kw2, p2; rep from * around.
Rnd 2 *Sl 1, dropping extra wrap, k4, sl 1, dropping extra wrap, p2; rep from * around.
Rnds 3–6 With B, *sl 1, k4, sl 1, p2; rep from * around.
Rnd 7 With B, *sl 1 to cn and hold to *front*, k2, k1 from cn, sl 2, sl next st to cn and hold to *front*, return first 2 sl sts to LH needle, k1 from cn, k2, p2; rep from * around.
Rep rnds 1–7 for sl st pat.

Note
Slip all stitches purlwise with yarn in back.

Collar
With A, cast on 120 sts using provisional cast-on method. Place marker (pm) for beg of rnd and join, being careful not to twist sts.
Work in sl st pat until piece measures 7"/18cm from beg, end with a rnd 7.
Next 2 rnds With A, *k6, p2; rep from * around. Bind off loosely in rib as established.

RUFFLE
Carefully remove provisional cast-on and place sts on needle. Pm for beg of rnd.
Next rnd With A, knit.
Next rnd With B, *k1, yo; rep from * around.
Next rnd Knit.
Rep last 2 rnds once more.
Work in St st in stripe pat as foll:
2 rnds A, 6 rnds B, 2 rnds A, 5 rnds B, 2 rnds A. Bind off loosely.

Finishing
With crochet hook and A, work 1 rnd of backward single crochet around lower edge of ruffle. ■

Gauge
24 sts and 32 rnds to 4"/10cm over St st using size 4 (3.5mm) needles.
Take time to check gauge.

Buttoned Cabled Cowl

A wide interlocking cable encircles this cowl that closes with six delicate buttons.

DESIGNED BY ANGELA TONG

■■■□

Knitted Measurements
Width
6"/15cm
Length
23½"/59.5cm

Materials
■ 1 3½oz/100g hank (each approx 307½yd/281m) of Cascade Yarns *Venezia Sport Multis* (merino wool/mulberry silk) in #207 frosted

■ One pair size 7 (4.5mm) needles
or size to obtain gauge

■ 6 buttons

■ Cable needle (cn)

■ Stitch marker

Stitch Glossary
12-st RC Sl 6 sts to cn and hold to *back*, k6, k6 from cn.
12-st LC Sl 6 sts to cn and hold to *front*, k6, k6 from cn.

Cable Pattern
Rows 1, 3, 5, 9, 13, 15, and 17 (RS)
Sl 1, k2, p4, k24, p4, k3.
Row 2 and all WS rows Sl 1, k6, p24, k7.

Row 11 Sl 1, k2, p4, 12-st RC, 12-st LC, p4, k3.
Row 18 Rep row 2. Rep rows 1–18 for cable pat.

Cowl
BUTTONHOLE BORDER
Cast on 68 sts.
Next row (WS) Sl 1, p to end.
Buttonhole row (RS) Sl 1, k1, *k1, slip this st back to LH needle and pass next 8 sts on LH needle over this st, [yo] twice, k the first st once more, k2; rep from * to end.
Next (dec) row (WS) Sl 1, *p2tog, [k1, k1 tbl] in first yo, then [k1, k1tbl] in 2nd yo, p1; rep from * to last st, k1—38 sts. Knit 4 rows, slipping first st of every row.
Next (set-up) row (WS) Sl 1, k6, p24, k7.

BEGIN CABLE PAT
Work row 1 of cable pat over 38 sts. Cont to work cable pat in this manner until row 18 is complete. Rep rows 1–18 eight times more. Then rep rows 1–9. Knit 6 rows for garter st button band. Bind off.

Finishing
Sew buttons to button band to correspond to buttonholes. ■

Gauge
23 sts and 30 rows to 4"/10cm after blocking over St st using size 7 (4.5mm) needles.
Take time to check gauge.

56

Smocked Belt

An obi-inspired belt boasts a flattering allover smocking stitch and I-cord ties for the perfect fit.

DESIGNED BY AMY POLCYN

Knitted Measurements

Length
17"/43cm
Width
6"/15cm

Materials

■ 1 3½oz/100g hank (each approx 307½yd/281m) of Cascade Yarns *Venezia Sport* (merino wool/mulberry silk) in #158 burgundy

■ One pair size 4 (3.5mm) needles *or size to obtain gauge*

■ Two double-pointed needles (dpns) for I-cord ties

Smocking Stitch

(multiple of 4 sts plus 1)
Rows 1 and 3 (WS) K1, *p1, k1; rep from * to end.
Row 2 P1, *sl 1 knitwise wyib, kfb, k1, pass slipped st over last 3 sts, p1; rep from * to end.
Row 4 P1, k1, p1, *sl 1 knitwise wyib, kfb, k1, pass slipped st over last 3 sts, p1; rep from *, end k1, p1.
Rep rows 1–4 for smocking st.

Note

Front panel should cover approximately ¾ of total waist measurement.

Belt

FRONT PANEL
Cast on 177 sts. Work in smocking st until piece measures 6"/15cm or desired width. Bind off in pat.

TIES (MAKE 4)
With dpns, cast on 4 sts.*K4; without turning work, slide sts to opposite end of needle to work next row from RS. Pull yarn tightly from end of row. Rep from * until cord measures 36"/91.5cm. Bind off.

Finishing

Sew one I-cord to each corner of front panel. To wear, cross ties in back, bring around, and tie at center front. ■

Gauge

42 sts and 40 rows to 4"/10cm over smocking st using size 4 (3.5mm) needles.
Take time to check gauge.

Solid & Striped Infinity Scarf

This graphic infinity scarf is worked in a tube and grafted at the ends—wear it long for drama or looped for warmth.

DESIGNED BY STEVEN HICKS

Knitted Measurements
Circumference
56"/142cm
Width
7"/18cm

Materials
- 2 3½oz/100g hanks (each approx 307½yd/281m) of Cascade Yarns *Venezia Sport* (merino wool/mulberry silk) in #130 light denim (A)
- 1 hank in #197 spring green (B)
- Size 6 (4mm) circular needle, 16"/40cm long, *or size to obtain gauge*
- Spare size 6 (4mm) or smaller circular needle for grafting
- Size G/6 (4mm) crochet hook
- Scrap yarn
- Stitch marker

Stitch Glossary
BYO Backward yarn over.

Provisional Cast-on
Using scrap yarn and crochet hook, chain the number of sts to cast on, plus a few extra. Cut a tail and pull the tail through the last chain. With knitting needle and yarn, pick up and knit the stated number of sts through the "purl bumps" on the back of the chain. To remove scrap chain, when instructed, pull out the tail from the last crochet st. Gently and slowly pull on the tail to unravel the crochet sts, carefully placing each released knit st on a needle.

Note
Piece is worked lengthwise in a tube, using the intarsia in the round technique; then the ends are joined to form the infinity scarf.

Scarf
With A, cast on 84 sts using provisional cast-on method. Place marker (pm) for beg of rnd and join, being careful not to twist sts.

Rnd 1 With A, k42, drop A (do not break) and pick up B (twist yarns to prevent holes), k42, sl marker, turn.
Rnd 2 With WS facing and B, yo, sl marker, p42, drop B and pick up A (twist yarns to prevent holes), p41, p2tog (last A st and yo), sl marker, turn.
Rnd 3 With A, BYO, sl marker, k83, ssk (last st of rnd and BYO).
Rnd 4 With A, knit.
Rep rnds 1–4 until piece measures 56"/142cm or desired length, end with a rnd 2.
Break yarn, leaving a tail approx 2yd/2m long for grafting ends tog.

Finishing
Weave in all ends except long tail. Carefully remove scrap yarn and place sts on spare circular needle. Holding needles parallel to each other with WS tog and striped sections matching, being careful not to twist the scarf, graft ends tog using Kitchener st. ■

Gauge
24 sts and 30 rnds to 4"/10cm over St st using size 6 (4mm) needles.
Take time to check gauge.

58

Lacy Loop-Edged Shawl

A geometric lace pattern is bisected by a column of eyelets
and softened by a looped crochet edging.

DESIGNED BY ANNIKEN ALLIS

■■■◻

Knitted Measurements
Width along upper edge
54"/137cm
Height at center
25"/63.5cm

Materials
■ 2 3½oz/100g hanks (each approx
307½yd/281m) of Cascade Yarns
Venezia Sport (merino wool/mulberry silk)
in #178 deep sea

■ Size 4 (3.5mm) circular needle,
32"/80cm long, *or size to obtain gauge*

■ Size E/4 (3.5mm) crochet hook

■ Stitch markers

Spine Pattern
(over 4 sts)
Row 1 (RS) K1tbl, k2tog, yo, k1tbl.
Row 2 P1tbl, p2, p1tbl.
Row 3 K1tbl, yo, SKP, k1tbl.
Row 4 Rep row 2.
Rep rows 1–4 for spine pat.

Notes
1) Slipped sts at beg of rows are worked
purlwise wyif.
2) Shawl is worked back and forth in
rows. Circular needle is used to
accommodate large number of sts.
Do not join.

Shawl
Cast on 10 sts.
Set-up row (WS) K3, place marker (pm),
k4, pm, k3.
Row 1 (RS) Sl 1, k1, yo, k to marker, yo,
sl marker, work row 1 of spine pat
over 4 sts, sl marker, yo, k to last 2 sts,
yo, k2—4 sts inc'd.
Row 2 Sl 1, k1, p to marker, work next
row of spine pat over 4 sts, sl marker,
p to last 2 sts, k2.
Row 3 Sl 1, k1, yo, k to marker, yo,
sl marker, work row 3 of spine pat
over 4 sts, sl marker, yo, k to last 2 sts,
yo, k2—4 sts inc'd.
Row 4 Rep row 2.
Rep rows 1–4 twice more—34 sts.

BEG CHART 1
Row 1 (RS) Sl 1, k1, work to rep line,
work 13-st rep once, work to end of
chart, cont spine pat as established over
4 sts, work to rep line, work 13-st rep

once, work to end of chart, k2.
Row 2 Sl 1, k1, work to rep line, work
13-st rep once, work to end of chart,
cont spine pat as established over 4 sts,
work to rep line, work 13-st rep once,
work to end of chart, k2.
Cont to work chart in this manner until
row 26 is complete—52 sts inc'd.
Rep rows 1–26 four times more, working
2 additional 13-st reps on each side of
the spine pat when each 26-row rep is
complete—294 sts.

BEG CHART 2
Row 1 (RS) Sl 1, k1, work to rep line,
work 13-st rep 11 times across, work to
end of chart, work next row of spine pat,
work to rep line, work 13-st rep 11 times
across, work to end of chart, k2.
Row 2 Sl 1, k1, work to rep line, work
13-st rep 11 times across, work to end of
chart, work next row of spine pat, work
to rep line, work 13-st rep 11 times
across, work to end of chart, k2.
Cont to work chart in this manner until
row 22 is complete—338 sts. Do not
break yarn.

CROCHET EDGING
With RS facing, insert crochet hook into
first 4 sts, yo and pull through all loops

Gauge
19 sts and 34 rows to 4"/10cm over chart pat using size 4 (3.5mm) needles.
Take time to check gauge.

Lacy Loop-Edged Shawl

CHART 1

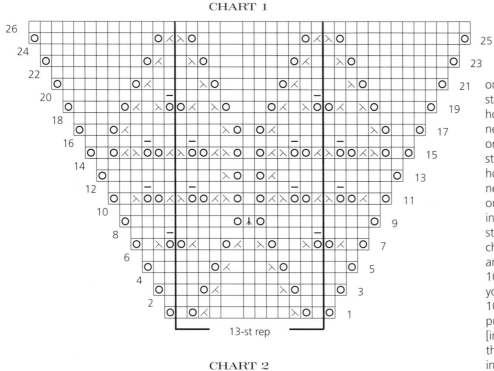

13-st rep

CHART 2

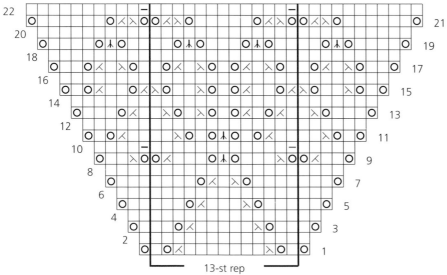

13-st rep

on hook, ch 10, [insert hook into next 6 sts, yo and pull through all loops on hook, ch 10] twice, [insert hook into next 7 sts, yo and pull through all loops on hook, ch 10, insert hook into next 6 sts, yo and pull through all loops on hook, ch10] 11 times, [insert hook into next 4 sts, yo and pull through all loops on hook, ch 10] twice, remove marker, insert hook into next 4 sts (spine pat sts), yo and pull through all sts on hook, ch 10, [insert hook into next 4 sts, yo and pull through all loops on hook, ch 10] twice, [insert hook into next 6 sts, yo and pull through all sts on hook, ch 10, insert hook into next 7 sts, yo and pull through all sts on hook] 11 times, [insert hook into next 6 sts, yo and pull through all sts on hook, ch10] twice, insert hook into last 4 sts, yo and pull through all sts on hook. Fasten off.

Finishing

Wet block, pinning shawl to measurements and pinning each crochet chain to shape. Let dry. ■

STITCH KEY

☐ k on RS, p on WS

─ p on RS, k on WS

⧄ k2tog

⧅ SKP

◎ yo

⋏ S2KP

Two-Color Lace Scarf

A dainty lace pattern gets an extra boost of beauty from contrast-colored dots.

DESIGNED BY MANDA SHAH

Knitted Measurements
Width
approx 6¾"/17cm
Length
approx 72"/183cm

Materials
■ 2 3½oz/100g hanks (each approx 307½yd/281m) of Cascade Yarns *Venezia Sport* (merino wool/mulberry silk) in #101 white heaven (MC)

■ 1 hank in #177 orchid haze (CC)

■ One pair each sizes 6 and 7 (4 and 4.5mm) needles *or size to obtain gauge*

Stitch Glossary
Dec 5-1 Ssk, k3tog, pass ssk over the k3tog–4 sts dec'd.

Scarf
With larger needle and 2 strands of MC held tog, cast on 29 sts.
Change to smaller needles and single strand of MC.
Next row (WS) K2, p to last 2 sts, k2.
Row 1 (RS) With MC, k2, k2tog, *[yo, k1tbl] 3 times, yo, S2KP; rep from * to last 7 sts, [yo, k1tbl] 3 times, yo, ssk, k2.
Row 2 and all WS rows through row 14 With MC, k2, p to last 2 sts, k2.
Row 3 With MC, k2, k3tog, *yo, kfb, k1, kfb, yo, dec 5-1; rep from * to last 8 sts, yo, kfb, k1, kfb, yo, k3tog tbl, k2.
Row 5 With MC, k2, k1tbl, *yo, k2tog, k3, ssk, yo, k1tbl; rep from * to last 2 sts, k2.
Row 7 With MC, k2, k1tbl, *yo, ssk, k3, k2tog, yo, k1tbl; rep from * to last 2 sts, k2.
Row 9 With MC, k2, k1tbl, *k1tbl, yo, dec 5-1, yo, k2tbl; rep from * to last 2 sts, k2.
Row 11 With MC, k2, k1tbl, *yo, k1tbl, yo, S2KP, [yo, k1tbl] twice; rep from * to last 2 sts, k2.

Row 13 With MC, k3, *kfb, yo, dec 5-1, yo, kfb, k1; rep from * to last 2 sts, k2.
Row 15 With CC, k3, *sl 3, [k1, yo, k1] in same st; rep from * to last 6 sts, sl 3 wyib, k3.
Row 16 With CC, *k3, sl 3 wyif, k3; rep from * to last 3 sts, k3.
Row 17 With MC, k3, *SK2P, sl 3 wyib; rep from * to last 6 sts, SK2P, k3.
Row 18 With MC, k3, *[p1, yo, p1] in same st, sl 3 wyif; rep from * to last 4 sts, [p1, yo, p1] in same st, k3.
Row 19 With CC, k3, *sl 3 wyib, p3; rep from * to last 6 sts, sl 3 wyib, k3.
Row 20 With CC, k3, *sl 3 wyif, p3tog; rep from * to last 6 sts, sl 3 wyif, k3.
Row 21 With MC, knit.
Row 22 Rep row 2.
Row 23 With MC, k2, k3tog, *yo, k3tbl, yo, dec 5-1; rep from * to last 8 sts, yo, k3tbl, k3tog tbl, k2.
Row 24 Rep row 2.
Rep rows 1–24 until piece measures approx 72"/183cm from beg, end with a row 23.
With larger needle and 2 strands of MC held tog, bind off in pat. ■

Gauge
17 sts and 28 rows to 4"/10cm after blocking over St st using size 6 (4mm) needles.
Take time to check gauge.

60

Cable and Bobble Mittens

Long lines flow from cables at the wrist up to delicate bobbles,
elevating these mittens to sophisticated heights.

DESIGNED BY PAT OLSKI

◀■■▭

Knitted Measurements
Hand circumference
above thumb
9"/23cm
Length
12½"/31.5cm

Materials
■ 1 3½oz/100g hank (each approx
307½yd/281m) of Cascade Yarns
Venezia Sport (merino wool/mulberry silk)
in #187 sage

■ One set (5) each sizes 1 and 2
(2.25 and 2.75mm) double-pointed
needles (dpns) *or size to obtain gauge*

■ Cable needle (cn)

■ Scrap yarn

■ Stitch markers

Quick Tip
If you have trouble knitting 5 stitches
together through the back loops when
making the bobble, use a crochet hook to
draw the yarn through the stitches.

Stitch Glossary
MB (make bobble) ([k1, p1] twice, k1)
into same st, turn, p5, turn, k5tog tbl.
2-st RPC Sl next st to cn and hold to
back, k1, p1 from cn.
2-st LPC Sl next st to cn and hold to
front, p1, k1 from cn.
2-st RPC tbl Sl next st to cn and hold to
back, k1tbl, p1 from cn.
2-st LPC tbl Sl next st to cn and hold to
front, p1, k1tbl from cn.
3-st RPC Sl 1 st to cn and hold to *back*,
k2, p1 from cn.
3-st LPC Sl 2 sts to cn and hold to *front*,
p1, k2 from cn.
7-st LPC Sl 3 sts to cn and hold to
front, [k1tbl, p1] twice, k1tbl, p1,
k1tbl from cn.

Twisted Rib
(over an even number of sts)
Rnd 1 *P1, k1tbl; rep from * around.
Rep rnd 1 for twisted rib.

Right Mitten
CUFF
With larger dpns, cast on 58 sts. Place
marker (pm) for beg of rnd and join,
being careful not to twist sts. Knit 9 rnds.

Gauge
26 sts and 41 rnds to 4"/10cm over St st using larger needles.
Take time to check gauge.

Cable and Bobble Mittens

60

BEG TWISTED RIB
Work 13 rnds in twisted rib.
Next (cable) rnd P1, k1tbl, p1,
[7-st LC, p1] 3 times, *k1tbl, p1; rep
from * to last st, k1tbl.
Work 6 rnds in twisted rib.
Rep cable rnd.
Work 5 rnds in twisted rib.
Change to smaller needles. Work 7 rnds
in twisted rib.
Next rnd [P1, k1tbl] 14 times, p1,
pm for palm, k29.
Work 7 rnds even in pat, working in rib
as established over 29 sts and working in
St st (k every rnd) over 29 palm sts.
Change to larger needles.

BEG CHART
Rnd 1 Work chart over 29 sts,
sl marker, k29.
Cont to work chart in this manner
through rnd 33, AT THE SAME TIME,
when rnd 2 is complete, shape thumb
gusset as foll:

THUMB GUSSET
Inc rnd Cont to work chart pat on 29 sts
for back of hand, k2, pm, M1, k1, M1,
pm, work to end of rnd.
Next 3 rnds Work to marker, sl marker, k
to marker, sl marker, work to end of rnd.
Next (inc) rnd Work to marker, sl marker,
M1, k to next marker, M1, sl marker,
work to end of rnd—2 sts inc'd.
Rep inc rnd every 4th rnd 4 times more—
13 gusset sts between markers.
Work 3 rnds even.
Next rnd Work to marker, place next
13 sts on scrap yarn for thumb, work to
end of rnd.
Next rnd Work to held sts, pm, cast on
5 sts, work to end of rnd.

Next rnd Work to marker, sl marker, k5,
work to end of rnd.
Next (dec) rnd Work to marker,
sl marker, SKP, k1, k2tog, work to end
of rnd.
Next (dec) rnd Work to marker,
sl marker, SK2P, work to end of
rnd—58 sts.
When chart is complete, rep rnd 33 over
back of hand until piece measures
10½"/26.5cm from beg, or 2½"/6.5cm
less than desired length from unrolled
cuff to tip of middle finger.

SHAPE TOP
Rnd 1 (dec) P2tog, p to 2 sts before
marker, p2tog, sl marker, ssk, k to last
2 sts, k2tog—4 sts dec'd.
Rnds 2–4 P to marker, sl marker,
k to end of rnd.
Rep rnds 1–4 six times more, then rnd
1 once—26 sts.
Rnd 20 [P1, p2tog] 4 times, p1,
[k2tog, k1] 4 times, k1—18 sts.
Rnd 21 [P2tog] 4 times,
[k2tog] 5 times—9 sts.
Break yarn, leaving a long tail.
Thread through rem sts and cinch
tightly to close.

THUMB
With larger needles, pick up and k 4 sts
along thumb opening, M1, place 13
thumb sts on dpns, M1—19 sts. Divide
evenly on 3 dpns and pm for beg of rnd.
Work even in St st until thumb
measures 2"/5cm.
Next (dec) rnd [K to 2 sts before end of
dpn, k2tog] 3 times—3 sts dec'd.
Rep dec rnd 3 times more—7 sts. Break
yarn, leaving a long tail. Thread through
rem sts and cinch tightly to close.

Cable and Bobble Mittens

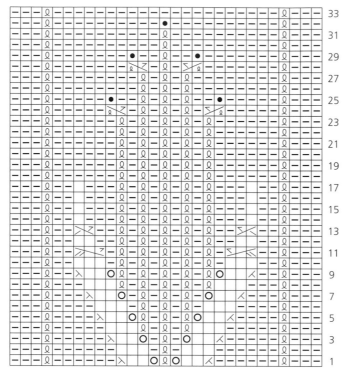

33
31
29
27
25
23
21
19
17
15
13
11
9
7
5
3
1

Left Mitten

Work as for right mitten to thumb gusset.

THUMB GUSSET

Inc rnd Cont to work chart pat on 29 sts for back of hand, k to last st, pm for thumb, M1, k1, M1.

Next 3 rnds Work to thumb marker, sl marker, k to end of rnd.

Next (inc) rnd Work to marker, sl marker, M1, k to next marker, M1, sl marker—2 sts inc'd.

Rep inc rnd every 4th rnd 4 times more—13 gusset sts between markers. Work 3 rnds even.

Next rnd Work to thumb marker, place next 13 sts on scrap yarn for thumb, cast on 5 sts, pm for new beg of rnd.

Next rnd Work to thumb marker, sl marker, k5.

Next (dec) rnd Work to thumb marker, sl marker, SKP, k1, k2tog.

Next (dec) rnd Work to thumb marker, remove marker, SK2P—58 sts.

Complete as for right mitten. ■

STITCH KEY

☐	k on RS, p on WS	⧄ 2-st RPC
−	p on RS, k on WS	⧅ 2-st LPC
⧄	k2tog	2-st RPC tbl
⧅	SKP	2-st LPC tbl
O	yo	3-st RPC
Ω	k1 tbl	3-st LPC
●	make bobble (MB)	

174

index